I Hardly Ever Wash My Hands

The Other Side of OCD

I Hardly Ever Wash My Hands

The Other Side of OCD

J.J. KEELER

PARAGON HOUSE

Published by
Paragon House
1925 Oakcrest Avenue, Suite 7
St. Paul, MN 55113
www.ParagonHouse.com

Library of Congress Cataloging-in-Publication Data

Keeler, J. J., 1978-
 I hardly ever wash my hands : the other side of OCD /
by J.J. Keeler. -- 1st ed.
  p. cm.
 Summary: "Describes the challenges of a young woman living with obsessive compulsive disorder (OCD) and how OCD impacts her ability to live a normal life, including her harming obsession, fear of AIDS, and other issues, approaching this serious subject with humor"-- Provided by publisher.
 ISBN 978-1-55778-892-4 (pbk. : alk. paper)
 1. Keeler, J. J., 1978---Mental health. 2. Obsessive-compulsive disorder--Patients--Biography. I. Title.
 RC533.K435 2012
 616.85'2270092--dc23
 [B]
                        2011048220

The paper used in this publication meets the minimum requirements of American National Standard for Information Sciences—Permanence of Paper for Printed Library Materials, ANSIZ39.48-1984.

Manufactured in the United States of America
  10 9 8 7 6 5 4 3 2 1

To my mom who always said I'd write a book. To my dad who never told me the definitions of words and made me consult a dictionary instead. And to my husband for pretty much everything.

ACKNOWLEDGEMENTS

First and foremost, I'd like to thank Rosemary Yokoi of Paragon House. Without her kindness, enthusiasm, and patience this book would not be possible. A special shout out to Perry Weissman, the first and only writing teacher I've ever had to declare the five paragraph essay to be a waste of time. I'd also like to thank Stephanie Antoun, Liz Osband, and Victoria Hoehn for reading the first draft of this book and telling me it was brilliant even when it wasn't. And finally a huge thanks to all the friends and family members whose names and stories I used in this book. You know who you are and you know that I love you.

Contents

PROLOGUE
Welcome to the Other Side ix

CHAPTER 1
When AIDS Came Out 1

CHAPTER 2
The Bomb in My Teddy Bear 19

CHAPTER 3
The Rules 35

CHAPTER 4
Ashes to Ashes 53

CHAPTER 5
The Dating Game 68

INTERMISSION
It's Not Always OCD 82

CHAPTER 6
A Bump in the Road. 85

CHAPTER 7
A Talk with God 101

CHAPTER 8
The Belly of a Babe. 118

CHAPTER 9
First Do No Harm 134

CHAPTER 10
I Know This Sounds Crazy 154

CHAPTER 11
Dear Friend, ...158

PROLOGUE

Welcome to the Other Side

SOMETIMES I WONDER IF I ever would have killed myself.

I guess the fact that I'm still here gives me my answer. But, if I'm being honest, I'd have to say I don't know.

It's not like I planned it or anything. It's not like I ever knelt in the upstairs closet with a gun to my head, caressing the steel trigger and willing myself to pull it.

It's not like I ever sat in a lukewarm bath with a cold razor to my wrist, daring myself to start to cut on the count of three.

It's not like I ever stood on a roof with my toes hanging over the edge, wondering what it would feel like to fly.

No, I never planned on suicide. But, then again, I'm not a planner.

If it ever were to happen, I knew it would only come in a moment of desperation, a split second decision that would last for all eternity.

There would be no preparing, no thinking through. I would write no note leaving nothing to no one. Instead, I'd make a decision almost without realizing, the way someone decides to sip a drink of water or scratch an itch behind their head.

Sometimes I wondered if it would happen. Other times, I wondered when.

Why am I telling you all this? You're not my therapist. Unless my therapist is reading this. In that case, hello.

You might know someone like me. You might be someone like me. I didn't plan this for my life.

It's not like I went to career day at school and thought, *Being a lawyer sounds neat. Being a doctor sounds cool. But, I really want to grow up to be in the depths of despair.*

There was a time when suicide wasn't even in my vocabulary; it was something I never thought I'd consider. But, I never thought I'd be someone with a mental illness either.

It's odd being someone with a mental illness, just like it's odd talking about suicide. Yet it's easy to see they go together, like bacon and eggs, or first dates and outbreaks of acne.

Sometimes I wonder why we never talk about this kind of thing in everyday conversation. We talk about other things that are revealing. We talk about having ingrown toenails or being afraid of haunted houses. We admit to watching *Jersey Shore*.

But suicide often falls through the cracks. I can understand why: it's not exactly a popular dinner subject. *This salmon needs salt and also I'm thinking of sticking my head in the oven.*

My eleventh grade health teacher often talked about suicide; he was against it. He probably would have lost his job had he been an advocate. Suicide, he always said, was a permanent solution to a temporary problem. I believed this to be true.

But then my mental illness, my OCD, came along and my viewpoint changed dramatically. One moment I couldn't fathom why people would ever kill themselves. The next moment I understood.

I know it could be worse; things can always be worse. I could be schizophrenic or delusional. I could have a disease where I am compelled to eat buttons or one where I'm afraid of falling asleep. Still, no mental illness is a picnic—unless you tend to picnic in the depths of Hell.

You might be wondering how bad it can be, this OCD of mine.

Maybe you're thinking I wash my hands a little too often, I organize things a little too thoroughly, I make sure my house is a little too clean. But, the truth is, I do none of those. OCD has another side.

Allow me to explain. One of my closest friends is a man named Kelley. He is a Japanese-Mexican American with a shaved head, a penchant for electronic cigarettes, and a killer poker game. We often laugh because most people, upon hearing his name, assume that he is a young, red-headed lass who just arrived from the Emerald Isle.

In that way, OCD is like Kelley: it is not always what it seems. Sometimes, it can even be the opposite.

The entertainment industry and media portray OCD as a disease marked by order, sanitation, and routine. Sometimes an extreme fear of germs is thrown in too. When I see this, I laugh and laugh. But then, I stop laughing, because, really, it's not that funny.

Don't get me wrong. OCD is often a disease marked by a debilitating obsession of all the above things, but that's only part of the story. Sometimes it's none of the story.

Take me, for instance. In many ways I am the antithesis of the typical OCD sufferer. My house is not clean. My socks are not matched. My jeans are as suitable for cleaning my hands as the water flowing from the bathroom faucet. I haven't balanced my checkbook since 1998. I am known for being easy going.

Even as I write this, we have a mouse living under our stove. I'm not worried. I'm not anxious. In fact, I don't really care at all. I'm hoping one of our cats will scare him off or that he will simply decide to see himself out. But, if not, that's fine. I'm sure he'll move on eventually.

A lot of people with OCD would be sent into a panic by a mouse, or, more likely, by the fact that their house was messy enough to invite a mouse. But, I simply see him as part of suburban living.

And, I call him Clyde.

I might not be like many of the others. I'm a different kind of OCD sufferer, but I am a sufferer nonetheless.

Looking back, it seems I've always had it, the way I've always had blue eyes or a tendency to tap my feet to a song's beat.

It hasn't always been the same. It has jumped around from an obsession with AIDS to an obsession with rules, from an obsession with praying to an obsession with morals.

Even as a child, it festered. Sometimes, I'd step on a crack and fear arriving home to find my mom hunched over with a broken back. Our eyes would meet, and she would know I was to blame. I'd be grounded and my inheritance would be divided between my sisters.

Other times, I'd quickly react to the pinch of my skin and squish a mosquito sucking blood from my arm. Then I'd spend that summer night on my knees praying for that insect to go to Heaven. This changed when a mosquito gave my cousin Quinn meningitis on a family vacation to Florida. After this, I became obsessed with squishing any mosquito I saw. If I didn't, I would leave them free to sicken someone else.

Sometimes, I'd leave school and see a friend being picked up by someone I didn't know. I'd obsess over whether this person was a relative, or a stranger wanted in six states for kidnapping. Other times I'd refuse to sing along to Bon Jovi's "Shot through the Heart," believing if I did, I would somehow be shot through *my* heart.

All of this was bothersome, but it wasn't devastating. It was like a dull headache you sometimes forget you have. It wasn't until my early twenties that it became a migraine.

This was the year my OCD played its trump card, the year it turned my thoughts into true harming obsessions.

It was life changing, these harming obsessions. I woke up one morning worrying about my term paper on Oliver Wendell Holmes. I went to bed that night worrying about tossing a baby down a mall escalator as onlookers watched in horror. I never worried about Oliver Wendell Holmes again.

In fact, the onset of harming obsessions was so devastating that I now look at my life in the same manner as people who've become paraplegics or lost their hearing: before it happened, and after.

I'm getting ahead of myself. I forget that not everyone has these obsessions. You may have no idea what they are.

By definition, they sound so simple: those of us with harming obsessions have an obsessive fear of harming others. But, they are much more complex.

Some of us might obsess about harming our loved ones, some of us might obsess about harming strangers, some of us might even obsess about harming our pets or ourselves. Some of us simply obsess about harming everyone.

There is often no limit to how this harming can take place: a gun, a knife, a freak accident, a vehicle, our own hands. With harming obsessions, everything and anything can be imagined into a weapon.

One day we may worry about stabbing our child with a letter opener as they sleep; the next day we might fear grabbing a plastic sack and suffocating an elderly woman as she selects avocados at the supermarket. We may obsess about throwing hot coffee on a coworker or running over a group of trick-or-treaters with our mother's minivan. We might even worry about our inactions, fearing that our failure to remove a rock from a walking trail will cause a hiker to trip and fall to his death down a treacherous canyon.

On one level we know these obsessions aren't a reflection of reality. We tell ourselves not to worry. But, the obsessions persist and pester. They build in our heads until we yearn for reassurance the way a junkie yearns for a fix.

Then we take this reassurance any way we can.

We check our child's bed for blood. We return to the supermarket to make sure the elderly woman is alive and breathing. We search our coworker's face for signs of scalding. We read the newspaper for reports of hit and runs. We remove the rock from the path and toss it into the woods. We call the police just to make sure nothing happened.

We ask those around us if they've noticed anything. We try to ignore their quizzical looks and furrowed brows, but we don't tell them the truth. We know they wouldn't understand.

Often, we don't even realize what we are going through is a mental illness.

I didn't.

When I started having harming obsessions, I concluded that harm was something I *wanted* to do. I imagined myself a ticking time bomb, a serial killer in the making. It would be only a matter of time before my skin was shed like a cicada to reveal a monster underneath.

Soon, my picture would be on a most wanted poster. Hopefully, I'd be having a good hair day.

This was when I contemplated suicide. I felt killing myself would prevent me from hurting others—it would save someone else.

The first few months of these obsessions, I feared harming anyone who was near me. Men twice my size, women with mace, people with black belts in karate: my OCD told me I might hurt them all.

It was in the winter of 1999 that my harming obsessions reared an even uglier head and focused mostly on children. I was in the worst place at the worst time when this happened: Disney World.

That day, it was the Unhappiest Place on Earth.

Why my obsessions focused on kids was not clear at the time. I'd always loved kids and was very good with them. I worked in a daycare. I thought about becoming a teacher. The last thing I ever wanted to do was hurt anyone, especially a child.

Now I know that my obsessions focused on kids because, in my mind, harming a child was the worst thing a person could do. It was worse than harming an adult. That, in a nutshell, sums up OCD's mode of operation: whatever the sufferer finds the most repulsive, this disease latches onto and doesn't let go.

I still can't believe I was at Disney World when this shift occurred. *Really nice timing, OCD. Thanks for that.*

I was walking through the park that day, frozen with the fear and stress that I would hurt someone. I wanted to cut out my brain, or gnaw off my hands. I wanted to do anything that would render me incapable of harm.

I walked across a bridge, afraid that I'd pick up a child and toss her into the pool below. I stood in line, afraid I'd push a child in front of the moving tea cups. I boarded a boat, fearing I was going to throw a child overboard. I rode Thunder Mountain and spent the entire time wondering what the hell was wrong with me.

I even worried about children harming themselves and me standing by like a statue, emotionless and still.

By noon, I was totally paranoid of being a killer. I had never been more afraid in my entire life.

It's hard to explain what this feels like. It's a mixture of feeling out of control, scared shitless, and empty. It's like morphing into someone new, jumping aboard a runaway train and waving a tearful goodbye from the railway car while the person you thought you were stands alone on the platform.

Later that day at Disney World, I broke off from my family and spent hours retracing my steps, looking for any signs of harm—police tape, mayhem, bodies covered in white linen sheets. I got on my stomach and parted the murky waters near the submarine ride, trying to quiet the mind that was telling me a child was drowning.

It was evening when I saw a pair of policemen headed my way. I felt my heart drop into my gut, the way it does when someone jumps out and startles you or you slam on the brakes to keep from hitting a deer. They walked by me with little more than a nod and a smile. Part of me expected to be arrested.

Yet, in the middle of madness, I did have one reprieve.

I was near the end of this awful day when I walked into one of Disney's restaurants. Out of nowhere, a toddler ran over to me, smiled, and hugged my leg. It felt like she was telling me that I wasn't what I feared.

I have no idea who this toddler was and I never saw her again. But she saved part of me that day.

Hopefully, this book can save part of someone else.

So, this is my story.

Welcome to the other side.

CHAPTER 1

When AIDS Came Out

I CAN'T TELL YOU HOW many times I've had AIDS. I've probably had it more often than the average person has had a common cold or a sinus infection. I've had it more often than the average child has had strep throat or the average athlete has had a muscle pull. I've had AIDS more times than I can count.

In fact, I can't even remember all of the times I've gotten it. Some of them stick in my mind, but others have wafted away, replaced by more current infections. Yet I do remember where I was when AIDS came out. I remember it with the same tragic recall of where I was when the Challenger exploded and when the Twin Towers fell.

AIDS came out when I was in third grade. I walked in on my parents talking about it. I wish I had walked in on them having sex instead.

The whole thing began because of a fight I had started with my twin sister Kim.

She and I shared a bedroom (even though our *younger* sister had her own room). Since we were twins, my parents kept up the stereotype and bought us bunk beds.

We used these bunk beds to sleep, of course, but we also used them for entertainment. We wrote on them. We jumped off them. We occasionally took our very unhappy dog up to the top of them. We sometimes used them to practice for the Doublemint Gum commercial we were sure we'd be on.

These bunk beds were also used as a prop in a game we had

invented, a game called Dandruff. I was using them to play this game on the night that AIDS came out.

The game was easy to play: when Kim went into our closet to find her pajamas, I climbed onto the top bunk and waited for her to come out.

When she did, I began rapidly dragging my hands across the ceiling, digging in my fingers so pieces came off.

I gladly watched the little white flakes sail through the air. Some fell straight down while other overzealous ones floated and twirled, blown in formation by the nearby heat vent. I smiled widely as several flakes came to rest in my sister's hair. Then I made fun of her for having dandruff.

We played Dandruff at random, sometimes a few times a month, sometimes a few times a week, but always to our parents' disapproval. According to them, our game would cause a hole in the ceiling and allow bats and spiders to come down through the attic.

A few months prior to this, Kim had conned me into letting her sleep on the top bunk for (in her exact words) "the rest of our lives." This left me unafraid of a hole—if bats and spiders did come down they'd land on her. I figured the screaming would give me time to escape.

Still, I knew I'd get in trouble if my parents found out we were playing. I decided to sneak into the kitchen and grab a trash bag— the evidence needed to be disposed of.

I didn't usually sneak out of my bedroom and into the kitchen, but when I did, the manner was always the same. I'd slink down the hall, and try to get past my parents as they sat in the living room watching television. With each step, I'd stop to listen for signs of movement. The only sound I usually heard was my heart pounding against my ribs, knocking so hard I was worried my mom would answer the front door, expecting to find a neighbor in need of a cup of sugar.

But this time it wasn't my heart pounding that drew my attention. Instead, it was the television program echoing off the living room walls. I could tell from the enthusiasm of the on-air voices that my parents were watching the news: only news anchors could make themselves sound excited over things like the Dow Jones or the results of the President's latest colonoscopy.

In the past, I had always found the news boring and depressing and I waited for the day when it would be cancelled, yanked off the air, and replaced with sitcoms, those that starred Soleil Moon Frye and taught the world that all problems could be resolved with a group hug.

But on this occasion, a story caught my attention. This story talked of a disease called AIDS, a disease that compromised the immune system and left people with no resistance to death. According to the news anchor, this disease had been quietly circulating around various parts of the world for years.

I was trying to digest what this meant, when I heard my dad tell my mom that he was surprised I'd never been tested for AIDS because of a blood transfusion I'd had years earlier. The instant I heard this, everything changed. I forgot all about the trash bag and the white ceiling flakes—flakes that had moments earlier mounted into an Everest-like pile in my imagination. Suddenly, I had bigger worries: I had AIDS.

After overhearing this conversation, I began to watch the news and listen to the rumors in hopes of finding out exactly what AIDS was and how people got it.

All the kids in school said AIDS came from monkeys, and I found myself taking this to heart, believing it could have started with King Kong and Ann Darrow's love affair, an affair where I imagined they kissed, cuddled, and showed affection just like other typical couples.

I worried fervently about my most recent trip to the zoo,

wondering if the monkey who blew me a kiss could have somehow given me the virus.

The adults in my life denied this, squashing the monkey rumors running rampant through third grade. According to them, AIDS was only transmittable through sex (whatever that was), dirty needles, and blood transfusions.

It was true I had a blood transfusion during a childhood heart surgery. But despite this being the obvious risk factor, the fear I received AIDS from a transfusion didn't concern me much at the time and I quickly forgot all about it. Instead, there was a different risk that consumed me. This was the risk of dirty needles.

I thought "dirty needles" simply meant needles with dirt on them, so I was certain things like nails, thumbtacks, and pine needles all paved the way for AIDS transmission. And I soon realized, as I began shooting beady-eyed glares in the direction of every pin cushion I saw, AIDS had me surrounded.

Even with this realization, my obsession with AIDS did not take off right away. The foundation was laid, but the proverbial house wouldn't be constructed until I was in fifth grade and attending a school carnival.

I spent my grammar school years at an elementary school in suburban Colorado. It was home of the Roadrunners, even though the only roadrunner I've ever seen was in New Mexico. The school was typical: the cafeteria served hot dogs with the same consistency as rubber, the smell of Bactine and crayons lingered in the air, and a school carnival was put on by the PTO every August.

This carnival was a time of year where children's feet were happy and excited as they pounded against the school parking lot. Warranting the excitement, this carnival had everything: games, food, a dunk tank used to sink our gym teacher and a giant inflatable castle I desperately wished my parents would move us into after selling our boring, non-inflatable house.

The carnival was designed so that kids could win all sorts of prizes. Some of the games gave prizes to everyone, things like animal shaped erasers and cheap plastic yo-yos. But some games, such as the cake walk, allowed only one winner.

The cake walk was one of those games that involved no skill. This was enough to assure me I could win.

I didn't really know what the cake walk involved, but I lined up anyway. When the music began, I followed the kid in front of me and began walking around in a circle. I figured the game was like musical chairs, only without actual chairs.

When the music stopped, I followed the eleven other kids and searched for a number to stand on.

I looked down and saw I was standing on number 6, a number I had hated since the age of six when a waitress yelled at me for unpotting a plant in a Mexican restaurant. I quickly looked over for any available numbers and saw number 1 staring back at me, its top looking like a curled finger calling me over. I willed my legs to move, but they ignored me and instinctively suggested I stay put.

When the teacher read the number she had drawn from a hat, it took me a few seconds to realize I had won. I smiled shyly and concluded to myself that I was the best cake walker in the whole school.

My prize was a poster of dogs playing poker.

"It's a famous portrait," the teacher mumbled as she placed the poster in my hands.

"A famous portrait," I repeated, all the while believing that it was just a poster demonstrating what dogs really do when they are left alone.

I went home to hang it on my bedroom wall.

Kim and I shared a room until we were eleven and tried unsuccessfully to divide it into sides with a strip of tape stuck across the floor. Our room's layout wasn't meant for this and our sides inevitably merged together, like grains of sugar dissolving in a glass of iced tea.

Kim wasn't fond of posters and preferred to hang up shopping bags from posh department stores in both a tribute to her fashion sense and an omen of the credit card debt that would meet her in college. She decorated our walls with bags from places like Guess and Esprit.

Sometimes, when she wasn't looking, I added bags to her collection from places like 7-11 and Grocery Warehouse.

Until now, there was only one other poster I'd ever wanted to hang in our room. It was a picture of Steve Watson, a Denver Broncos receiver. Kim made me hang it in the closet.

But this time around, I vowed to proudly display my winnings.

I entered my room, poster in hand, with determination and strength, half expecting my stuffed animals to clap and cheer, supporting me in my mission. I figured I would hang the poster up in the most obvious spot in the room, somewhere it could serve as a conversation starter. *Oh, that poster? Where'd I get it? Well, let me tell you how good I am at carnival games.*

Taking a thumbtack from my sister's collage, I smiled as a Benetton bag fell to its death, disappearing underneath the bottom bunk. I dropped the thumbtack into my pocket and climbed on top of the dresser.

After unrolling the poster against the wall and guessing it was straight, I reached into my pocket. Almost immediately the thumbtack—a dirty needle—stuck my finger. Once again, I had AIDS.

I got AIDS another time when I was fourteen. As an eighth grader, I was a typical student: I hated junior high. I hated the cliques, I hated the yellow lights in the gym, I hated how people always wrote unflattering pieces of gossip inside the stalls of the girl's bathroom, and I hated how I always feared those pieces of gossip would be about me. More than anything, I hated how our school song was comprised of lyrics that didn't rhyme.

In a daydream I often had, I was asked to rewrite the school song. After a few brainstorming sessions, sessions in which I suddenly knew how to play piano, I wrote a song that delighted my choir teacher and caught the attention of a record producer. This eventually led to a Top 40 hit, standing as the only school song in history to top the charts and have a large cult following.

Yet, my vision remained just a vision, and I was forced to muddle through middle school like everyone else.

A few weeks into my eighth grade year, I befriended a girl named June. We had known each other for a couple of years but had never really been friends until we found ourselves sitting next to each other in second period algebra, using one another to solve for X.

June dyed her hair black and dark purple, sometimes using hair dye and sometimes using Kool-Aid. She wore ripped t-shirts and jackets with patches representing heavy metal bands. She snapped her gum during class and drew peace signs on her jeans with black markers. She was someone cool. But, apparently, I was among the few who thought this.

Since June was shunned by the majority of our preppie, rugby shirt-wearing eighth grade class, and since I was that girl who once accidentally got an unused maxi pad stuck to the outside of my school binder and walked around the halls for hours before noticing, June and I needed each other. And so, we became friends.

Towards the end of eighth grade, she sat right behind me in a class called "Outdoor Living," a class teaching extreme outdoor survival skills. This class taught us how to light a kerosene lamp and that wrapping a towel around our heads would help trap in warmth.

Our teacher was a soft-spoken man with a bushy beard and

piercing blue eyes. While he talked, many of us passed notes to each other or played games on our calculators. June, however, used this time to draw things on herself. She usually drew smiley faces on her arms or wrote boys' phone numbers on the inside of her hands, retracing each number several times with a ball point pen.

During one particular class, she was feeling inspired and gave herself a makeshift tattoo. She used a needle she had stolen from her diabetic cousin and scratched a heart into her arm. When she was done, she looked at her bleeding tattoo and tapped me on the shoulder.

I didn't respond, too wrapped up in a segment about grizzly bears, so she poked me in the back with the needle.

She poked me so lightly there was no way the needle even broke my skin. Yet, I suddenly began feeling a cool sensation trickle down my back. It was a familiar sensation, one I felt whenever I popped a zit or coughed hard enough to reason my exploded lung was bleeding into my stomach.

I immediately assumed the needle had ruptured something: a vessel, a vein, an artery. Whatever it ruptured, one thing was certain: I was bleeding profusely. I hurriedly excused myself from class.

I rushed through the hall towards the bathroom, certain people would stop in their tracks to stare at my blood-stained shirt. Some would point and laugh, others would whisper to each other, commenting that the red on my shirt didn't match my shorts. The more intuitive students, realizing I was losing pints per minute, would hold out their arms and offer me O positive blood on the condition I do their homework for a month.

I reached the bathroom, locked a stall, and yanked off my shirt. As I stared at it from all angles, even standing on the toilet seat to view it directly under a fluorescent overheard light, I noticed my clothing didn't contain a single ounce of blood, not even the slightest speck.

I stared at the shirt for several minutes, jumping off the toilet whenever I heard someone coming. I stared and stared as if blood would magically appear like invisible ink or a tank full of sea monkeys.

After a few minutes, I was satisfied my shirt contained no blood. This led me to be pretty certain my back wasn't bleeding. But, I had to know for sure.

The bad thing about being obsessed with my back bleeding, aside from the fact I was obsessed with my back bleeding, was there was no real way to check; I couldn't see my back.

I thought about asking the next girl who walked into the bathroom to check for me, but my asking of a question like that was sure to spread through the halls like water from an open hydrant, leaving me waving a neon freak flag from the school's roof. I tried turning around and looking at my back in the mirror, but my body wouldn't contort enough for me to see.

Finally, I decided to lean my back up against the wall of the bathroom stall, reasoning that if my back was bleeding, an imprint of blood would remain, displayed on the stall like biological graffiti.

The wall revealed no signs of blood, and I decided I was not in need of a transfusion; I would live to see another day. But, the instance this satisfaction set in, I felt a sinking feeling in the pit of my stomach. And then it hit me: *What if June has AIDS?*

By this time, I no longer worried about getting AIDS from needles simply because they had dirt or germs on them. But, I did worry about getting AIDS from needles that contained the blood of someone else, someone such as June.

Still, I was fairly certain June didn't have AIDS, and besides, I assured myself, the needle probably didn't even break my skin. I was safe.

A few weeks later, my confidence diminished.

It was the last week of eighth grade. The reverberations of lockers slamming shook the school halls and kids signed yearbooks, begging each other to stay in touch always and forever.

I handed my yearbook to June. When she returned it, I immediately read what she wrote.

I was expecting a note of sentiment like: *Dear Friend, you are the greatest person I know. I am sure I will see you in high school before you go on to Harvard.* Instead, I found a note containing a bunch of swear words.

Every sentence June had written contained the word "fuck." What was worse, she had also wished me a "sex-filled summer." She had written fuck and mentioned sex. I immediately came to one explanation: she was a hooker and she had AIDS. And, with her blood soaked tattoo needle, she had given it to me.

I worried about June giving me AIDS all summer. If that wasn't enough, I also began to worry that I had gotten AIDS from my childhood blood transfusion.

The year of my blood transfusion was the year I was born, 1978. It was years before HIV became an epidemic. But I knew it was possible that AIDS, even before it was discovered, existed in silence like some sort of reclusive creature hiding in the crevices of old Colorado mining towns. I figured the odds I received blood tainted with HIV were about one in five billion, but that one chance made it possible. That one chance was all my brain needed to turn the possible into the probable.

My mom told me I could get tested if I was so worried about it. But I refused; if I did have it, I didn't want to know. She then suggested that I call my aunt to speak to her about my concerns. She was a retired nurse and someone, my mom thought, who could talk some sense into me.

RANDOM OCD FACT NUMBER 1:
Approximately 3 million people in
the U.S. are believed to have
OCD.*

Auntie Bev told me that it was highly unlikely, though, I noted, she didn't say impossible. She also told me I was smart for being concerned about it. *Screw being smart, I just wanted to be virus-free.*

When I reached high school, my obsession with AIDS began to wane and I started to believe no earlier instances had really infected me, though I was not 100 percent sure.

It was about this time that Kim became a full-fledged hypochondriac and convinced herself she had all kinds of diseases.

Instead of feeling hypocritical, I embraced my sister's hypochondriacal tendencies by shaking my head in disgust and rolling my eyes whenever she mentioned a new disease. I reasoned that Kim's paranoia was worse than mine because she refused to exclude a single disease from her list of possible diagnoses; I waited for the day when she diagnosed herself with prostate cancer.

By far, Kim's two biggest concerns tea partied between appendicitis and brain tumors. These diseases occurred randomly, sometimes popping up while she searched the clearance rack at the mall, and sometimes coming on while she passed the rolls at dinnertime.

---

*National Institute of Mental Health (NIMH)

They lasted a few hours and then, defying medical science, healed themselves.

I didn't want to be as paranoid as my sister, nor did I want to be consumed with disease, and so I began seeing my AIDS obsessions for what they were: ridiculous.

Besides, it was high school and there were a million other typical things to be obsessed with. I was obsessed with getting good grades, I was obsessed with hanging out with my friends, I was obsessed with boys, and, for one particular month after reading Franz Kafka's *The Metamorphosis,* I was obsessively worried about going to bed as a human and waking up as a giant bug.

High school was a honeymoon for me. Because of all the angst that came packaged in the foam peanuts of the teenage years, I almost forgot all about AIDS.

Almost, but not quite.

When I got to college, I started to get AIDS all over again. I began to worry I did in fact get AIDS from many of the earlier occurrences, including attending junior high with what I imagined was a plethora of hookers.

I also began to imagine getting AIDS from everyday, typical activities.

I got it while dining at an Italian restaurant when the waiter, a ridiculously skinny man clad in a white apron, waited for my attention to be diverted by breadsticks, pricked his finger with a butter knife and allowed drops of his blood to flow into my Diet Coke. I got it when my dog, outside chewing on the body limb of an HIV infected person, came inside with blood all over her mouth and began to lick a cut on my leg where I had nicked myself shaving an hour earlier.

I got it when I went hiking in Las Vegas and lost my footing. Trying to regain my balance, I cut my hand grabbing for a tree branch, the same tree branch someone with HIV had undoubtedly cut their hand on moments earlier. I got it when I went inside an outhouse at a park and saw, in addition to the usual odor, a toilet seat sprayed with urine. Though I decided not to use it and immediately left, I got AIDS anyway.

On a few occasions, I got it from talking to people. They'd annunciate a particular word and specks of spit would fly from their mouths, sailing through the air and looking for a place to land. Though this spit always fell directly down, letting gravity take its course, I often imagined these specks, mixed with blood, somehow finding a way into my mouth.

When I had these thoughts, I'd wipe my tongue with the sleeve of my shirt. If the thought was particularly intense, I'd have to rush to the nearest bathroom and wash my mouth out with soap. Then I'd do it again. And again.

Sometimes I got AIDS once a month, sometimes it was once a week. Sometimes I wouldn't worry about it for months, other times I'd get AIDS four days in a row.

Eventually, I became obsessed with getting AIDS by merely walking, something I did frequently along the city streets.

The late John Denver wasn't talking about drugs when he wrote the song "Rocky Mountain High," but the cities in Colorado, like many cities in America, had IV drug users. I obviously wasn't one of them, being instead the type of person who lied awake at night wondering if I took too much Dimetapp. But, I was sure a lot of people were. I was also sure these drug users threw their dirty needles onto city streets. And I was certain these discarded syringes, filled with HIV-infected blood, were all over the sidewalks, stuck in erect positions in the concrete, with their needles pointing towards the sky.

In my mind, the streets of Colorado and everywhere else were littered with syringes cemented in rows like a Walk of Fame for disease. Traveling by foot without stepping on dirty needles was inevitable—it was like stepping on an ant hill without killing any ants.

Most of the time I walked anywhere, I would have to carefully study the path in front of me, making sure it was free of the needles I feared. I'd often walk while looking down, just in case a needle darted out in front of me like a nervous-looking rabbit crossing the highway.

When I did step on something—a rock, a branch, a lump in the pavement—I'd have to go back and make certain I didn't actually step on a needle.

Sometimes people walked by as I intently examined a square of sidewalk for syringes. They'd shoot me a curious look and I'd tell them that I was looking for a dropped quarter. Looking for loose change seemed more acceptable than looking for an imaginary syringe.

I was once walking my dogs near my parents' house when I found an actual syringe.

I was always seeing weird things in this area—once I saw a horse in someone's backyard, another time I saw a German Shepherd running around on the roof of a house, once I even saw a giant pig walking along the green belt. But this was the first time I ever saw a needle.

I saw this needle from afar—it was probably ten or twelve feet ahead of me—and immediately walked across the street, determined to avoid it at all costs. Even then, I couldn't be certain I hadn't stepped on it. I bent over and checked the soles of my shoes, looking for tiny needle marks.

I walked past the area, telling myself over and over again that surely it was just a needle that a diabetic had dropped. The more I tried to convince myself, the less convinced I became.

After walking about fifty yards, I got an image in my head of a child picking up the needle and accidentally pricking herself. She would get AIDS and it would be my fault. I couldn't leave it. I had to go back.

I devised a strategy. I found a large tree branch and planned to use it to push the needle into rocks. I'd then use the branch to gather more rocks, completely covering the needle. This way, no kids would see it and no one would be tempted to play with it.

I was walking towards the needle when I spotted a man picking it up off the ground. He did this with ease, like he was picking up a penny or a dropped car key. I assumed it was his. Or maybe he too was protecting children from the lethal virus.

Sometimes, my obsessions would subside and I'd forget about AIDS and all the ways I had received it. But, soon, something would happen and I would be reminded, and, just like that, my obsessions would start up again.

I would hear about HIV or AIDS on the news and I would be reminded. I would watch a television drama with a character who was HIV positive and an intrusive thought would invade. *Oh yeah, I almost forgot, I've got that too.*

I would see the movie *Philadelphia,* or hear the theme song playing on the radio, and then spend an hour looking for purple lesions all over my body, the kind of lesions that covered the chest and face of Tom Hank's character.

When I thought there was nothing worse than having AIDS, I finally thought of something: *what if I gave AIDS to others?*

Since I was in college, I lived in close proximity to other people. We had few boundaries between us: we shared utensils, shared bathrooms, even shared suckers and bubble gum. Because of this, I was certain I had given AIDS to those with whom I lived. Unbeknownst to them, they were living with a murderer, or perhaps a manslaughterer (it depended on how the jury would rule).

Once this obsession set in, I could no longer take the anxiety and I got tested. I drove to a drugstore in the middle of the night with my neighbor Andrea, a good friend whose eye rolls served as the voice of supportive reason.

As we drove in her blue Honda, Mary Chapin Carpenter sang "Grow Old Along With Me" on the radio and I prayed it was a sign I would indeed grow old along with everyone else.

We entered the drugstore and began looking through all the aisles, whispering to ourselves like two kids about to shoplift. The HIV home testing kits were in what I called "The Aisle of Embarrassment," a row containing everything people never wanted to be seen purchasing—HIV testing kits, tampons, laxatives, adult diapers, hemorrhoid cream.

I quickly grabbed a testing kit, covering it with the sleeve of my jacket so others couldn't see what I was buying, and immediately went to pay.

As I handed the kit to the cashier, I thought for sure he would call for a price check over the intercom the way cashiers did in movies when teenage boys were nervously buying condoms. Instead, he just rang it up as if I were purchasing something as normal as a bottle of soda or a bag of chips.

When we got home, I read the instructions.

The test was simple. All I had to do was register my test ID number by phone, prick one of my fingers, and place a few drops of blood on a collection card. After sealing the card, and putting it in the provided envelope, I placed it in the mail. The instructions said to call in three days to retrieve my results.

I called after three hours, before my test kit even left the mailbox.

Calling nearly every hour on the hour for the next three days, my test finally came back negative. I was greatly relieved and felt like the world's heaviest shoulder pads, shoulder pads I had been wearing since the height of their fashion in the mid-1980s, had been lifted off.

This relief was short-lived.

Within an hour I began to worry the testing facility made a mistake. I imagined a lab technician, wearing a white coat and a pencil protector, fumbling with samples of blood.

Sleep deprived after staying up late the night before to watch a *Star Trek* marathon on TV, the technician had trouble staying awake, nodding off a few times and hitting his wire-rimmed glasses on the eye piece of the microscope.

As he dealt with numerous samples, stopping only to sip ineffective coffee out of a Captain Kirk mug, he began to lose focus, mixing up the samples in the process.

This fear kept nagging at me, even after I called the testing place several times and heard the same automated message tell me my result was negative.

So, I called back again and pressed zero: I needed to speak with a counselor.

The counselor assured me that everything was triple checked and no mistakes were made, and that, yes, they were definitely FDA approved. After talking to her at length and asking numerous and redundant questions, I was confident the test was accurate. I was also confident I was going to be the inspiration behind their company's newest slogan: "If you have OCD, please don't buy our product, and also please lose our number."

I thought getting tested for HIV would quiet my fears. But, it just lit a flame under my obsession. It was a form of checking, one I did often.

By the end of my twenties, I had been tested more than twenty-five times without having a single formidable risk factor. And, with each negative test, there was—and still is—a sense of doubt. The fear of AIDS for me, much like the disease for those who actually have it, will probably never go away.

Nowadays, the obsession ebbs and flows. The vast majority of the time, I don't worry about it at all. My mind has moved on to other things. But it is always there, sitting behind the scenes of my brain, waiting to be called to center stage.

In case you are wondering about Kim, she is still a hypochondriac. Just the other day she had appendicitis, again. She cured it by going out drinking.

I, on the other hand, have never had appendicitis. I've never had a brain tumor either (I should probably add a "knock on wood" right here just for safe measure). This leaves me to confidently declare that while my sister is paranoid, I'm not.

She's had everything.

I've only had AIDS.

CHAPTER 2

The Bomb in My Teddy Bear

I ONCE HAD A TEDDY bear who tried to kill me. I was eight years old.

I'm not talking about a bear who came to life like the doll from *Child's Play*. Even *I'm* not that crazy. I'm talking about a teddy bear who tried to kill me with a bomb planted inside him. He had some help, from humans, of course.

I remember the day the bear and I met as vividly as I remember my wedding day, but I don't remember how my fear of bombs began.

Maybe it began while watching the television shows that made starting your car and having it blow up seem commonplace. Maybe it began when we learned of air raid sirens in history class. Maybe it began the day my cousin Travis convinced Kim and me that the Russians, bombs in hand, were invading his Oregon neighborhood while we were there for a visit. My aunt drove us around for two hours as we looked for them from the backseat of her station wagon.

Whatever the reason, I was scared of bombs, and believed they were everywhere.

Living in Colorado, this fear wasn't warranted; I wasn't exactly surrounded by explosives. I had a better chance of encountering a magical prairie dog than I ever did a land mine. But, this logic didn't matter. It rarely does with OCD.

In 1986, this fear spread into my toy collection. This is the year there was a bomb in my teddy bear.

This bomb-toting teddy bear would not have entered my life if it wasn't for one person: my father.

My father was hard to figure out, like I had been given a Rubik's Cube for a parent. There were obvious things about him—he was a great admirer of Pepsi products, for instance, and never let anyone drink from his can—but he was also a bit of a conundrum. He was funny, but quiet, smart, but technologically challenged. While moral, goofy, and Republican were all words I could use to describe him, the one word I often used was "cheap."

I can still remember standing barefoot on the cement floor of our garage, watching him fix my Nike tennis shoe. Ignoring the fact that my shoe's stitching had completely come undone, duct tape—highly visible duct tape—was my father's way of avoiding the purchase of a new pair of shoes. He wrapped the metallic strip of tape around my shoe twice, tore it with his teeth and sent me off to second grade (this did not sky-rocket me to popularity among my elementary school peers as quickly as you might think).

In the mornings, he often poured the remaining crumbs from a box of Cheerios and the remaining crumbs from a box of Cornflakes into a single cereal bowl. I would stand there in disgust, watching him search for any other nearly depleted food item he could include in my cereal casserole. I hoped he wouldn't notice the half-eaten bologna sandwich sitting in the icebox or the quarter inch of pickle juice remaining in a jar in the front cupboard. He'd add the final contents of a box of Grape-Nuts, pour in some milk and ask with a satisfied smile, "There, now doesn't it feel good to know we aren't wasting food?"

When heading into Denver, he always refused to pay for parking. I asked him once why we had to park so far away from places like hospitals and convention centers.

"I'm not going to pay a quarter to park inside a parking garage when I can park outside for free," he said. "Besides when I was a boy

I walked everywhere." I'd roll my eyes as he continued saying that his walks were always accompanied by uphill battles in both directions and always, always took place during raging blizzards—even when he lived in Puerto Rico.

My father was cheap in many areas, yet there was one area where he was anything but. This was the area of stuffed animals.

Stuffed animals made my father a compulsive shopper, like a kid in a candy store filling his pockets with gumballs and his mouth with jaw breakers. There was something about stuffed animals that drew him in.

Whenever my sisters or I were sick, we'd receive a stuffed animal. Whenever any of our cousins came to visit, they'd receive a stuffed animal. Whenever my father wanted to be romantic with my mother, she'd receive, and return, a stuffed animal. To my father, stuffed animals were the answer for everything. They solved all the world's problems.

I often imagined him as an American ambassador during the peace talks of World War I. While men in tailored suits smoked cigars and sat around a table discussing terms, my father would stand up wearing red suspenders and his nicest pair of jeans and say, "Forget the Treaty of Versailles—tell the Germans to just give us teddy bears." And with that, the first world war would be resolved.

For me, an avid tomboy, the stuffed animals my father bought replaced the dolls my sisters loved, the dolls I thought were way too girly.

My twin sister Kim and my younger sister Stephanie were content to live in a world of Mattel and spent many days locked in the basement. In between fighting over who had to be Ken and who got to be Barbie, they developed complex story lines. One of their most memorable stories involved Skipper coming to town and breaking up Ken and Barbie's marriage.

I had no interest in Ken and Barbie (or that slut Skipper) so I dedicated myself to my stuffed animals.

They were the ones I carried with me to school, they were the ones I put in the basket of my bike, they were the ones I accidentally left below the drinking fountain at Baskin Robbins while consumed with the tragedy of a hole in my sugar cone.

By the time I was eight, I had well over fifty stuffed animals. Because my father bought so many of them, I collected stuffed animals without intending to. I collected them as inadvertently as a college student collects books or a mutt collects fleas.

Even though I had so many of them, each stuffed animal had a name and each one had a story.

My favorite story involved the stuffed panda bear my father bought me from a posh toy store when I was five in return for the agreement I would stop biting my fingernails, a habit I continue to do this day.

Black and white and half my size, my father paid eighty dollars for it in 1983. This panda, or "Andy Pandy" as he was known in the inner circle (the inner circle consisting of Andy Pandy and myself), became my companion for years.

I dragged him to the park, I took him to school for show and tell, I made my mom offer him mashed potatoes at dinnertime so I could have him say things like, "No thanks, I'm stuffed."

Eventually, his destiny took a tragic turn, a turn to which most stuffed animals are not subjected. This epitomized when he became a sex toy for my 16-year-old dog and was repeatedly humped (especially when company came over). When people saw this dog-on-panda-action, they often chuckled nervously. "It's okay," I reassured them, "they're in love." (In case you're grossed out, they *really* were in love.)

And that's how I saw all of my stuffed animals. To me, they were real. You could have pointed to any one of them and I would have been able to tell you their story. *Spot is a Dalmatian purchased from a discount store in early summer of 1984. A Gemini, he enjoys long walks on the beach, thunderstorms, and being stuffed with Styrofoam.*

While every animal had a story, they weren't all good. Most of them were funny or heartwarming or even, as demonstrated by Andy Pandy's sad tale, slightly pornographic. But then there was the teddy bear filled with a bomb. He was the bad seed, the only one who tried to murder my family.

If you've had a teddy bear try to murder your family, you know exactly what I'm talking about.

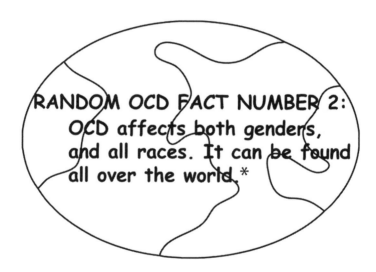

Before I can explain why this teddy bear tried to murder my family, I have to convey what my perception of murder was when I was growing up.

My neighborhood in Colorado was really a pretty safe place to live. Instead of crime, we had the typical characters found in Any Neighborhood, USA.

---

*National Institute of Mental Health (NIMH)

There were the Hanson boys who lived down the street. They had a Doberman Pinscher and a swimming pool. There was Rick and Lori, the couple next door who were waiting a few years to have kids. Kim and I helped them in this decision by frequently inviting ourselves over, addressing them by rhyming nicknames, and forcing them to sit and watch us act out commercials for Viva Cottage Cheese and Hi-C Fruit Juice.

There was the girl around three corners and down two streets who used to sing and dance to Madonna songs in her front yard. She once found Kim and me staring as she performed a rather stunning rendition of "Material Girl" and responded with a shout of "Fuck You."

Later in life, her house became known as "Fuck You Girl's House" and served as a cornerstone of providing directions. *Okay, to get to the store, turn right near the skinny oak tree and hang a left at Fuck You Girl's House.*

Living in this neighborhood, I was never worried about crime. Even the dark wouldn't scare me the way it was taught to scare kids and Kim and I never thought twice about sleeping with our bedroom window wide open to feel the breeze on warm summer nights.

But, this all changed.

One day, word started spreading about a person in a nearby town who had broken into a house and killed the people who lived there. No one knew who this person was and no one had any idea why these people were murdered.

My grandmother told me about it one afternoon, casually mentioning that there was a possible serial killer on the loose. At first, I took this the wrong way, simply wondering if someone was going around killing people with Captain Crunch or the sharpened edges of Chex Mix.

The news corrected me. It talked about a killer with no name, no face, no motive. With little to go on, my imagination filled the gaps.

I pictured him as an ax murderer, and imagined him running around with the ax on his shoulder, taking swipes at anyone he wanted.

Sometimes I imagined him killing inside public places: a mall bathroom or while in line for the roller coaster at the local amusement park. Other times I imagined him breaking into houses through bedroom windows or doggy doors.

Even though we had a doggy door in our kitchen, I wasn't that worried about the ax murderer fitting through it. It was a good sized doggy door, but too small for a grown man. I was certain if he tried to squeeze through, he'd get stuck halfway. My sisters and I would walk into our kitchen and see him lying there in hostile frustration. We'd scream for our parents, then hide behind my father as he dialed 9-1-1.

Instead, I was concerned about our bedroom window, a window only seven feet high off the side of our house.

The ax murderer coming in through this window wasn't my main concern. Instead, I was worried that he'd climb up on the firewood stacked outside, lift up his ax, and swing with all of his might. The ax would break the wire screen, then shatter the window pane. I imagined this done with the greatest ease, like a pair of scissors cutting through a thin piece of paper.

After destroying the window, the ax would swing freely inside our bedroom. It would slice up everything within its reach.

I was sure all of this was imminent, and it led me to live by one mantra alone: never sleep near the window.

That lasted for five days.

Kim was also afraid of the ax murderer. Before we got bunk beds, we had twin beds, one precariously placed next to the window, and one safely pushed against the opposite wall. This left us in a difficult situation. Neither of us wanted to sleep by the window, so we began sleeping in the same bed.

We hadn't slept in the same bed for more than a few nights when I began feeling a plucking sensation on the top of my head. I turned around to find my sister chewing on strands of my hair. The more I asked her to stop, the more of my hair she ate. I had no idea why anyone would want to eat someone else's hair, but I figured I had two choices: face my fears or go bald. Choosing the former, I began taking my chances with the window.

It wasn't until we got bunk beds months later that I finally got a good night's sleep—one that did not involve fear of waking up with missing legs in a pool of blood.

I had a picture of him in my mind. He was white with eyes so dark they looked black. Those eyes that could see into people, as if he was able to read the fine print written on your soul. Sometimes his hair was brown and sometimes it was gray. He had short stubble on his chin and dirty teeth and his eyebrows were so expansive they met in the middle, shaking hands like old friends.

When he smiled, which he rarely did, his smile was crooked, as if only the right side of his mouth was capable of happiness.

He lived in my imagination…and in our shed, which sat just to the right of our bedroom window. But each time I checked, I only found our snow blower, garden supplies, and broken tools. He was never in there.

The ax murderer faded from my mind eventually, but he was never truly gone, like a chicken pox scar that lightens but never leaves. His lesson always remained. He caused me, for the first time in my life, to realize that some people just weren't very good human beings.

This concept was always in the back of my mind, but I went on living my life and tried hard not to let it bother me.

Until there was a bomb in my teddy bear.

The day this teddy bear came into my life I was riding my bike home when I saw a garage sale out of the corner of my eye. On principle, I never bought stuff for myself at garage sales. I really didn't want to buy myself anything that was used. But, I had no problem buying used stuff for my family and so, I pulled over.

The garage sale didn't have much—a few chairs, some cassette tapes, a lamp with frilly tassels that hung down, outrageously colored silk shirts that reminded me of something my grandma wore, a Monopoly game with the thimble missing. There was nothing really interesting, and I turned to leave.

As I made my way down the driveway, a lady approached me with a yellow tattered teddy bear in her hand.

"Here," she said as she extended her arms and placed the bear within my reach, "you can have this, for free."

Now, I know the whole "strangers with candy" notion should have popped into my head—I shouldn't take things from people I didn't know. But, you have to understand. In my family, if you were offered a stuffed animal, you better accept a stuffed animal. I pictured my father beaming with pride as I accepted this stuffed animal the same way a military father beams with pride as his son joins the army.

Besides, this lady wasn't a complete stranger. I had seen her a few times shoveling the snow from her driveway or watering her lawn with her garden hose. She had a friendly smile and the biggest mane of blonde hair I had ever seen. Her hair was so big it looked as though she might actually have to tilt her head just to get through doorways.

In my memory her name was Linda, though in hindsight I'm not sure that was actually her name. Also in hindsight, I'm not sure she was actually a woman. It was, after all, a time when men and women often had similar hairdos; it was the 1980s and big hair had us surrounded.

After weighing the facts that she was offering a stuffed animal and that she *was not* necessarily a stranger, I decided there was no harm in accepting her offering. I thanked her, placed the bear in the basket of my bike and rode home.

When I arrived at my house, I rushed inside the living room and showed my father the teddy bear.

"That's nice, honey," he said in a way that meant, "I'm watching TV, so I have no idea what you just said."

Ignoring my father ignoring me, I carried the teddy bear into my bedroom and sat it on my dresser. As I stood there trying to think of names for it, I began to get a weird feeling about the bear; I began to think there was a reason a stranger gave me a stuffed animal free of charge.

Then, suddenly, it hit me. The reason was obvious: there was a bomb in the teddy bear.

I began to dissect the real story behind Linda and her family and the wholesome facade they presented in the form of a garage sale.

Their house was down the street and around the corner from ours. In terms of directions, it was located in between my house and Fuck You Girl's House. It was one story and white with brown trim and a porch swing out front.

I had been inside their house once before, once when the former owners had a Christmas party and I remembered the basement had windows blocked by filing cabinets and camping gear. It was the perfect place to make a bomb.

I imagined they picked me because my bike was so noticeable—it surely caught their eye as they looked up and down the street for a victim.

The bike had a severely yellow and blue banana seat complete with white wicker basket and—oh yes—a bell. It was a bike everyone made fun of and one I sometimes denied was mine until my father bought me a toy license plate with my name on it. He put this license plate on the front handlebars with wires that, no matter how hard I tried, wouldn't break.

I imagined Linda chuckling to herself as she saw me approach on my outrageous bike, the way a spider certainly chuckles to itself when it sees a fly heading for its web. After handing the teddy bear over to me, I was sure she gave the others a knowing glance and then, once I was out of sight, let out an evil laugh. And, I was sure it was only a matter of time before this teddy bear blew up and killed my whole family.

I sat on the edge of my bed and thought about ways to solve the problem.

I could sneak downstairs and put the teddy bear in the crevices of the storage room, but the storage room contained the furnace and that could cause an even greater explosion. I could place the bear in water and hope it ruined the bomb. But, I knew to get out of the pool during a lightening storm, so I was sure water wasn't a good idea.

I could put the bear outside, placing a pot or a pan over it to shield the blast. But, placing the bear outside could blow up my whole neighborhood. I could rip the bear open and try to diffuse the bomb myself the way I had seen on TV cop shows with men in flak jackets anxiously wondering whether to cut the red wire or the black one. But, I didn't know how. I was eight years old and I knew nothing about diffusing bombs. *My school system had failed me.*

As the night time sky went from blue to black, I knew I had no choice other than to wait till morning to solve my dilemma. But, if I was going to wait till morning, I was at least going to be smart about it.

I carefully picked the teddy bear up by the ears and placed it in our closet. Instantly, I felt a little better: I thought maybe my plethora of jean jackets—hard and starchy—would protect my family from the blow.

The next day I woke up to the feeling of my house shaking. Certain the bomb had just gone off, I was relieved to find the shaking was from my mom putting too many clothes in the washing machine, an act she practiced every Saturday of my childhood.

As I looked in the closet, I saw the teddy bear sitting in the very spot I had placed it the night before. Kim's bed was empty and I could hear her and Stephanie down the hall arguing over what cartoons to watch on TV.

I was grateful to have some time to myself, time I could use to form a plan.

As I sat cross legged on my bed, I carefully studied the bear.

It was an average-sized teddy bear with yellow fur and black eyes that looked old and scratched. It was also a lumpy bear, with the kind of lumps stuffed animals got when they were cuddled and laid on and given a lot of attention. Despite the teddy bear's violent behavior, it looked like a stuffed animal that had been greatly loved.

I began to search for a solution. My first instinct was to return the bear, just walk up to Linda and say, "I'm returning the bear because of its contents." I would use my fingers to place quotation marks around the word "contents" so Linda would know exactly what I was talking about. I would remain composed and calm as if I was returning the teddy bear with the same logic a person returns a shirt that's too small.

But, returning the bear would probably result in one of two things happening.

Linda and her family would frame me. They would call the police and say *I* was actually the one who had put the bomb in the teddy bear. I would go on trial and it would come out that I once kept quiet while witnessing my peers steal Skittles from the jar of my first grade teacher's desk. After hearing this, the jury would look at me in horror, with raised eyebrows and open mouths, and right then and there, I'd be ruined.

Or….

Linda and her family would kidnap me for uncovering their plot. They'd use Atari cables to tie me to a chair in their basement. I would sit there as they discussed what they were going to do with me.

After realizing they would have to either kill me or leave the country, they would decide to leave the country. In order to do this they would need money. They would write a ransom letter with cut outs from a JC Penney catalog and call my parents after the delivery.

"I don't know, that's A LOT of money," my cheap father would say. "Can I have some time to think about it?"

No, taking it back was not an option.

I thought about getting my stethoscope from my toy doctor's kit and listening to see if I could hear the bomb ticking, but I knew that wouldn't do any good. Obviously, it would be ticking.

I thought about wrapping the teddy bear in a protective barrier made of aluminum foil, but I wasn't sure if that would keep the bear secured, or just keep it fresh for tomorrow's supper.

I thought about taking the teddy bear to some rural area and throwing it away in a field. But that was no good. Someone would find it, take it home and then their house would blow up.

I thought about shoving it down one of the slits on the sidewalk curbs that led to the sewer. This way the bomb would be underground when it exploded. But the toxins from the bomb—there had to be toxins—would get into the city's water system and poison anyone who drank tap water.

There just had to be a safer way to get rid of a teddy bear with a bomb.

As weeks went by, I struggled to find a solution. As if the imminent explosion of a teddy bear wasn't enough for a kid to deal with, I soon started to fear that the bomb would never go off.

Of course that would have been a good thing; I hate an exploding teddy bear as much as the next person. But, I began to worry about Linda and her family coming by to finish the job they had started.

They'd wait until nightfall and then sneak into my backyard. The click of the gate handle would be drowned out by a passing car and the noise of gravel crunching under their feet would be expertly timed with the neighbor's barking dog. I wouldn't hear them coming.

They would approach my bedroom window where they'd be met by the ax murderer.

"This window's my territory," he would tell them, "but the smallest of you could fit through the doggy door around the corner."

And it would be that easy for one of them to get into our house. Or, maybe they wouldn't need to get into our house. Instead, they would just leave another bomb-filled stuffed animal outside our front door, or below my bedroom window.

Soon, I began engaging in rituals to protect my house from blowing up.

I checked for the footprints of criminals in the sand outside the back gate, as if criminals' shoes made tiny skull imprints instead of Nike signs. I routinely searched the outside of my house for stuffed animals. I looked in window wells and milk boxes, anywhere a stuffed animal could hide.

I stacked empty pop cans on the top of the back gate, believing an intruder would knock them over and warn me of their arrival. I covered the steps leading up to our doggy door with gravel, hoping the rocks would hurt the knees of any bad guys kneeling down to gain access.

I did this until I was satisfied nothing looked suspicious, all the while restraining myself from yelling, "What the hell do you think you're doing?" at the neighborhood kids who, stuffed animals in hand, came over to play.

After a few agonizing days, I figured no new bomb-filled stuffed animals were going to appear. But, that didn't solve my original problem: I still had the teddy bear.

Even though I continued to place it in the closet each evening, I was often afraid I would wake up in the middle of the night and it'd be sitting on my chest, staring down at me. Because of this, I started placing things like shoes or rolled up sweatshirts in the path that led to my bed. A few items of clothing would make it more difficult for this inanimate object to walk over to where I was sleeping.

Finally, after a few weeks with the teddy bear, I came up with a foolproof plan.

Next to the shed that housed the ax murderer sat my father's boat. It was a lime green boat my color-blind grandfather purchased years earlier. It smelled of shower tile and rubber and had a horn that sounded like a clown's nose. The boat was the solution.

My father often took this boat to Cherry Creek Reservoir, a few miles from our house. As legend went, this reservoir was created when a flood trapped a town under water in the early 1900s. When you trolled through the shallow parts, you could still see the tops of trees and houses and barns.

Sometimes I pretended people still lived in this town. They had normal lives and did normal things. They went to the market, and went to school, and rushed to the bank before noon on Saturdays. Only, they all wore flippers, and most of them had gills.

Cherry Creek Reservoir seemed like the perfect place to dispose of my teddy bear.

My father took us fishing there often, and I'd set my plan in action the next time we went. I would bring my teddy bear and tie something heavy, a brick or a rock, to one of its legs. Then, when my father wasn't looking, I'd toss the teddy bear overboard, like a stuffed animal that had betrayed the Mob.

As I waited for my father to mention he wanted to go fishing, something weird happened: my obsession with the bomb began to subside. I don't know if it was because I had a solution to my problem and that was all I needed, or if I just started obsessing about something else. Whatever the reason, I soon began to believe there was *not* actually a bomb in my teddy bear.

I still have a ton of stuffed animals. Throughout my childhood and adulthood, my dad continued to buy them for me. When I left home, my mom wanted to get rid of them, but my dad disagreed. He gave them to me and made me vow to "keep them in the family."

As a result, our house is filled with stuffed animals. There are hundreds on shelves, in closets, and on bedroom dressers.

I still have the teddy bear with the bomb.

More than two decades later, it hasn't blown up yet.

CHAPTER 3

The Rules

SOMETIMES I THINK PEOPLE WITH OCD view the world from inside a 1950s TV: we tend to see things in black and white. Things either have a right way or they have a wrong way. That is why OCD can often be marked by rules of being overly clean and meticulously organized. To be any other way is to be wrong.

People with OCD often have a ton of these rules they must abide by. Some have to hang their clothes in the closet sorted by color; a red shirt in between two orange ones might be enough to cause anxiety. Some have to arrange soup cans alphabetically, or sorted by things like salt content or brand. Some have to keep their homes so orderly that even a crooked picture frame or a misplaced shoe can cause a panic attack. A lot of people with OCD have these types of rules, rules of routine that keep their lives on track and in control.

As I mentioned earlier, I don't have these kind of rules. Instead, I run away from order like a cat fleeing a dog.

Not once have I ever been organized. Seriously, never. I practically came out of the womb having misplaced my umbilical cord.

In my younger years, I always told myself I'd get organized and stop being messy.

I promised myself in fourth grade that I would keep my pens and markers inside my Snoopy pencil box, with all their caps tightly screwed on. I told myself in high school that I would actually take notes during biology instead of drawing cartoon bears and monkeys in the margins of my notebook. I swore to myself that I'd keep my room clean, make my bed, and stop using the space behind my dresser as long term storage.

I eventually concluded that organization was just not going to take and I threw in the proverbial towel (or, more accurately, I threw the proverbial towel on the bathroom floor instead of hanging it on the hook where it belonged).

When my OCD exploded in college, I had still not become organized and my tidiness, or lack there of, had evolved into an art form. In fact, the college apartment I shared with my two roommates was marked by constant disorder.

In our defense—in case you are judging us or happen to work for the health department—the apartment we lived in was not all that nice to begin with. In Boulder, the truly nice places were reserved for millionaire business owners and kids with a bottomless trust (which, my parents repeatedly assured me, I didn't have).

Still, our place wasn't a total dump. We could have fixed it up and made it homey, but we opted for the opposite.

Instead of fixing our screen door when our neighbor's psychotic cat ran through it, we laughed. Instead of repairing the broken back lock with a kit from Home Depot, we simply kept the door secured with a giant stick. Instead of wiping up the squished spider that hung from our living room wall, we left the remains there as a warning for any of his little spider friends who were thinking of trespassing.

Our carpet was stained, our banister chipped, and our kitchen stove partially covered in some sort of noodle dish (circa 1998). Our cabinets were falling off their hinges and our bathroom mirror was broken so many times we were all looking at roughly forty-two years of bad luck.

Twice we were fined by the apartment manager for letting too many issues of the *Denver Post* accumulate on our front porch.

Once we were fined for not cleaning up the half-eaten crab legs the boys living above us had tossed off their balcony.

My roommates, Mollie and Courtney, were not especially tidy or organized either. But I was the driving force behind the mayhem, the eye of the storm. Courtney's mom even once asked me how Boulder County had not yet seized my room. I'm not sure if she was joking.

So, you see, I did not have the rules that some with OCD often have. Telling someone who had seen my college apartment that I had OCD was about as believable as telling them I had Jimmy Hoffa's body in the trunk of my car.

But that doesn't mean I didn't have other rules. There were areas where stringent laws did apply, areas as black and white as an Oreo cookie. One of these areas involved getting into trouble. This first manifested during elementary school.

I was not one of those kids who got in trouble often, especially not in school. I wanted nothing more than to impress my teacher and land in her good graces. But there were a handful of kids in my class who didn't share my enthusiasm for behaving.

There was the kid in first grade who brought a steak knife to school and showed it off during recess. When a teacher tried to confiscate it, he ran off and threw it down the sewer drain. None of us were allowed to go to recess until it was retrieved.

There was the kid who pulled the fire alarm to get out of a math quiz (he ended up taking it from the principal's office) and the kid who broke a plastic cafeteria tray over a fourth grader's head.

There were kids who called teachers names, kids who used house keys to scratch bad words into the desks of art class, and kids who wrote the names of US presidents on their tennis shoes, only to glance at them during history tests.

There was even an assault and battery during our third grade spelling bee when an overgrown eight-year-old, and frequent troublemaker, got reprimanded for disrupting. He retaliated by punching our vice principal in the face, knocking off his glasses and bloodying his nose. When I saw this happen, I was beyond stunned: I could not have been more shocked if a pterodactyl flew in and started playing the cello.

With an attempt to keep order, there was a system set up to enforce punishment for these kind of offenders. Some behaviors, such as the act of punching the vice principal (or really, any school official), bypassed the system and went directly to suspension.

But, most punishments stuck to the system like rubber cement on the back of construction paper.

The system was simple: during the first offense, the child's name was written on the chalkboard as a warning. More offenses warranted check marks. One check mark meant the child gave up recess, two check marks meant a trip to the principal's office, three check marks meant a call home, and four check marks meant a suspension.

Of the years I was in elementary school, I officially got in trouble once. It was in kindergarten.

I had been sitting on the floor for story time—sitting innocently, mind you—when a boy behind me yanked my hair. I turned around and told him to stop and my teacher, because I'd been talking out of turn, wrote my name on the board.

I was devastated.

I can still remember staring as my teacher glided the chalk across the board, leaving my name for everyone to see; it felt like pinpricks on my skin. Yelling from a mountain top that I was bad would have been more subtle.

That entire day I was certain, no matter where I was—swinging on the swing set, walking to the bathroom, climbing on the rope in gym class—people would see only one thing: someone who talked out of turn.

"Oh my," they would whisper behind my back, "there goes the girl who got her name on the board. She was talking out of turn and once I even saw her running—*Running!*—in the halls."

I walked around with an ache in the pit of my stomach, pitiful looks of shame coming from every face I saw. If I, at age five, had been a literary genius, I would have compared myself to Hester Prynne from the *Scarlet Letter.*

In reality, getting your name on the board was no big deal. It happened all the time for getting out of line, playing in the drinking fountain, or eating candy during class. It was no big deal, and yet, it stuck with me.

Why I remember it—something that happened almost three decades ago—is simple: even as a child, this was one of my "rules." Following it was an integral part of my life. There were two kinds of kids: kids who got their name on the board and kids who didn't.

After this single occurrence, I vowed to never get my name on the board again, and I never did. I even managed to evade getting my name on the board during fifth grade when our substitute teacher had some sort of mental breakdown and sent seven kids to the principal, before putting another ten in in-school suspension.

I'm not saying I was perfect (but you can, if you'd like). When you're a kid, not getting in trouble is like eating a peanut butter and jelly sandwich without getting any jam stuck to your fingers. It was almost impossible not to jump in puddles or climb up fences or do what all the other kids were doing just to make yourself fit in.

At home, I got in trouble on occasion and, other times, only got out of trouble because my sisters and I chose the art of blackmailing over the art of tattletaling. Kim and I once blackmailed our younger sister Stephanie for three years because she walked to a frozen yogurt shop when our dad instructed that she stay home.

Despite my talent for extortion, I was a pretty good kid.

In fact, one of the times I got in the most trouble—to the point of having law enforcement nearly involved—was for something I didn't do at all. It's also something I will never forget.

It happened the summer I was seven years old. Kim and I had spent all morning at our friend Kelly's house, playing in her front yard and eating Rice Krispies treats that her mom made the night before.

Right around lunch time, we decided we wanted Pudding Pops and sent Kim home to bring back three from our parents' freezer.

Kelly lived one street over from us, a mere two minute banana-seat bike ride. We expected Kim to be gone ten minutes at the most. When she didn't come back for twenty minutes, we began to grow impatient, wondering if she had pedaled off behind a tree and eaten all three Pudding Pops herself.

Finally, she came back empty handed and told me that we had to go home: she wasn't sure why, but we were in trouble.

None of us understood what was going on, but we pedaled home anyway.

We had barely reached our driveway when our across-the-street neighbor Laura came flying into the front yard. That's exactly how I remember her looking, like she was flying: an angry hawk diving towards unsuspecting field mice.

Laura immediately started yelling at us, flapping her arms and ranting widely. I waited for her head to start spinning.

She accused Kelly of calling her house and saying, "Kiss my ass," before hanging up. Kim and I, according to her, could be heard laughing loudly in the background.

Now, before I go on, let me explain what a ridiculous accusation this was. At the time, I was in second grade and had absolutely no idea what an ass was. No idea. I remember thinking that the word "ass" was the same as the word "ask;" the only crime that occurred was the use of improper grammar.

In fact, I never truly grasped the concept of a cuss word until a year later. This was when Stephanie began mispronouncing the word "truck," saying "tr-fuck" instead. My cousins and I would often ask her to say it, then we'd roll on the ground laughing.

To give you some further insight into my second grade naivety, this was a time when not only did I still believe in Santa, but I was also five hundred percent sure that Mickey and Minnie were real live giant mice, and not just Disney workers dressed in costume. I would believe this for four more years.

Despite these facts, Laura insisted we were guilty.

My father came outside as she was yelling. I don't think he knew what to believe (and, had we been the callers, I don't think he would have really cared). He didn't yell at us or threaten to wash our mouths out with soap. Rather, he told Kelly she should probably go home and told us to go play in the backyard.

Kim and I said goodbye to Kelly then wandered through the gate and began playing on our swing set.

Our swing set was green, old and metal, with swings made of cracked plastic and a teeter totter that neither teetered nor tottered. If anyone swung too high or too fast, the back legs came off the ground. I constantly worried this would cause the swing set to flip over, fatally harming a person—or a pet—in the process.

This worry had me so preoccupied that I didn't hear Laura's husband Ron open our back gate. He steamed up the pathway and stood on the lawn. Before we could say anything, he told us he was calling the cops (*what the tr-fuck?*).

You know the feeling you get when you wake up in a hotel room and it takes you a minute to realize where you are? That's what this was like. The entire event had me so confused that I wondered if I was dreaming. I had no idea why we were in so much trouble for an act we did not commit. There was one thing, however, I knew for sure: I wouldn't do well in jail.

I could picture it in my mind: I'd be assigned to a cell with a large, burly man, one whose entire right arm was covered in rose tattoos and hearts that read, "Mama." He'd have long oily hair and he would spit whenever he spoke. He'd ask why I was in jail and I'd meekly say it was for a prank call. He'd then smile a buck-toothed grin and tell me he was in for murdering a prank caller.

After Ron made his threat, he stood there waiting for us to admit our crime. But, we weren't going to own up to something we didn't do. We told him this: we didn't have anything to do with the prank. To his credit, he backed off and instead of pushing the issue, told us that if we said we didn't do it, he would believe us.

In the midst of all this, my mom came home from work. She was livid. But, not at us—she knew if we said we were innocent, we were. She was livid at Laura. She took Kim and me by the hands and walked across the street, determined to confront Laura at her home.

My mom rang the doorbell and Laura came to the door. What happened next still plays in my head like a movie.

My mom told her we hadn't done anything wrong and that she owed us an apology. Laura paused for a moment and I prepared myself to say, "No, no, it's okay. I forgive you."

But she didn't apologize. Not even close.

Instead, she called my mom a "fucking cunt." Years later, my mom told me that she had no idea what that even meant.

After this, my mom's relationship with Ron and Laura was non-existent. Even when Laura eventually apologized, the wound that had been ripped open wouldn't close. But my mom was also upset with my dad. His refusal to side with us, remaining indifferent on the sideline, left my mom feeling as though he chose Laura over his children. She was so irate with him that she packed our bags and we moved to my grandmother's for a week. She swore, up and down, that she and my father were getting divorced.

My mom's anger eventually subsided and she and my dad reconciled. It was around this time we learned from Ron and Laura's son that they had used the phone company to trace the prank back to two random teenage boys. They moved away three months later.

As a child, the effect this had on me was profound. It not only taught me that all hell can break loose when a child gets into trouble, but it also showed me that trouble wasn't reserved for the guilty.

For months, I was terrified I would pick up the phone to call my grandma or a friend and I would accidentally misdial. The person on the other end would mistake my wrong number for a prank call. They would hear me apologize and take it to mean something vile. Or maybe they would hear my hesitant breaths and take me to be one of those perverts known for heavy breathing. They'd erupt in anger and call the authorities. Once again, jail would beckon.

This fear caused me to dial as slowly and carefully as possible. Sometimes, I'd have a feeling that I'd misdialed and I'd have to hang up and start over. On more than one occasion, I hung up on my grandma, mistaking her voice for that of a stranger.

I knew, from a rational standpoint, that I couldn't really go to jail for a prank call. But, OCD is not driven by rationality; it is a disease where fear is the driver, while imagination sits shotgun.

Soon it expanded into other areas of my life.

Before I realized it, I became completely obsessed with making sure I didn't put myself in situations where trouble could be erroneously pinned on me. As you might guess, this proved pretty impossible.

RANDOM OCD FACT NUMBER 3:
OCD can be hard to recognize
when you don't know what you
are looking for.

The first few occurrences of these obsessions happened at my grandma's house.

While growing up, my sisters and I constantly took turns spending the night with her. This was a greatly coveted privilege.

At my grandma's, I had the toy box, and all its contents, to myself. I got to stay up until the end of *Hill Street Blues*. And I got paid three dollars for vacuuming her living room. Most importantly, while my parents instituted a "one junk food a day" rule, my grandma did not: chocolate milk and soda pop flowed freely.

I was at my grandma's house more times than I can count. But, two times stick out in my mind. These were the times I almost landed in jail.

The first instance occurred when I was eight and coloring in the family room. My grandma sat, as she always did, in her recliner, cigarette in one hand, TV remote in the other. I sat on her orange couch doing my best impression of—you might say—a young Monet.

I was adding the final touches to my masterpiece (one that would hang on my grandmother's refrigerator for three weeks straight!), when a blue crayon slipped from my hand and fell into the couch cushions. I reached down to find it and grabbed hold of a piece of paper instead. My curiosity peeking, I gave it a yank. It was stuck so I yanked harder. I heard a rip and felt the paper relax in my hand.

I looked down to see what it was and noticed a tag, like the kind found on a mattress. This tag read, "DO NOT REMOVE UNDER PENALTY OF LAW." Immediately, panic set in.

I imagined a sensory device on every upholstery item sold in America. Whenever any tag was removed, I told myself, authorities were automatically notified. A giant red button was pressed and a police team dispatched. It was only a matter of time before I would hear a knock at the door of 16319 W. Atlantic Place.

For several minutes I sat frozen, straining to hear the screech of a siren or the whirl of a helicopter. I looked over to see if my grandma had noticed, to see if she could be brought up on charges of abetting. Luckily, she was engrossed in an episode of *The Golden Girls* and didn't see a thing.

When no police came to the door, a bit of rationality crept in. Maybe, I told myself, upholstery sensors didn't exist. Maybe, I could just pretend it never happened. In the end, that was my solution.

If there was one thing my grandma did with authority it was drink coffee. The amount she drank every day assured me that she would have to pee at any moment. I was right.

A few seconds after she got up to use the bathroom, I ran to the desk in her living room and grabbed a piece of tape. I returned to the couch and flipped over its cushion. Then, I carefully taped the DO NOT REMOVE tag back to its original home.

When my grandma returned, I sat there innocently, a fake chuckle leaving my lips. Betty White, I told her, was hilarious.

Within a day or two, I knew the police weren't going to show up and arrest me, but that didn't stop me from remembering this occasion. It also didn't stop me from being extremely careful around all upholstery from then on. To this day, I can't see a DO NOT REMOVE tag without getting a little anxious.

Less than a year later, I was almost arrested again.

On the side of my grandma's house there was a small grove of apple trees. My grandma occasionally picked these apples to make pies or give to neighbors, but most of the apples fell off the trees into the rocks below.

At the age of nine, I believed my grandma was old....like really, really old. I didn't think she should bend or stoop or pick up any kind of fruit. So, I often removed these apples from the rocks for her.

I was engaged in this chore when the two girls who lived across the street ran over and started throwing leaves at me. They smiled and waved and hurriedly gathered another pile.

These girls were a few years older than me. They both had straight blond hair, identical facial expressions, and long, skinny legs. I always referred to them as "the sisters."

I sometimes played with them when I visited my grandma. We'd always gotten along so wonderfully that I didn't even hesitate to pick up a pile of leaves and toss them back in their direction.

I'd only thrown a leaf or two when the younger sister started complaining that I'd hurt her. I balked at her accusation, telling her that leaves didn't hurt. She paused for a moment, and then accused me of wrapping the leaves around one of my grandma's fallen apples. She ran and told her sister this very theory.

In no time at all, the older sister was in my face, yelling at me. I tried to tell her that I hadn't thrown any apples, but she wouldn't listen. Then, she said the six words that were like a death sentence to any nine-year-old, "We aren't playing with you anymore."

I was upset by the sudden disappearance of my playmates, but I was more upset by the unfounded accusation. I really *hadn't* thrown any apples. I was so upset that I ran back into my grandma's house and found solace in the living room chair.

I sat there, thinking about what had happened, when it hit me: *what if the sisters call the cops?*

They hadn't threatened to call the cops, but this didn't stop me from thinking that they might. Then, once again, I began picturing myself in a jail cell. This time, I imagined, I would be in a cell with a cannibal. I would tell him I was in jail for throwing apples and he would tell me that apples were his favorite food. Second to people.

My grandma eventually came looking and found me in the chair, coiled in a ball. She coaxed me into telling her what had happened. Then, she marched outside and gave the sisters a piece of her mind.

The sisters responded much more favorably to my grandma than me. The younger one relented and agreed that maybe no apples had been thrown. This reassured me, but not 100 percent. Part of me still wanted—in writing—a statement that they wouldn't involve law enforcement.

Over the next few years, I continued to be a strict follower of these rules. This was unfortunate timing: I was approaching the teen years, a time when rebellion was at the top of the To Do List.

The group that I ran with during this time was made up of girls somewhat testing the limits of authority. Polly sometimes snuck out of her bedroom window, Kelly was often grounded, Teresa had friends over when her mom said she couldn't, and Amy sent lying letters to radio stations in an attempt to get free New Kids on the Block tickets.

Being a pre-teen came with a lot of pressure to fit in and it seemed, at this juncture of life, being bad was synonymous with being cool.

I wasn't willing to be overtly rebellious. But I wasn't a saint. Sometimes I would tell my parents only smidgeons of the truth. Other times I'd peek at my Christmas presents before they were wrapped. Sometimes I'd even tell my dad that I went straight home after school when I really went to Polly's house. Here, we'd spend hours watching owls as they sat on the roofs of townhomes across the field. We were always amazed that they never moved (and we learned years later that they were plastic).

While I wasn't perfect, there was a line I wouldn't cross. But sometimes I pretended to cross it happily.

One incident that sticks in my mind involved a local supermarket.

This supermarket was about a half mile from our house. We could easily reach it without crossing any major streets or leaving the boundaries of our neighborhood. For these reasons, we were allowed to walk there whenever we wanted.

Kim and I often went to this supermarket with a friend or neighbor. One reason for our frequent visits was that this store had several types of candy people could sample for a dime.

This candy was stacked in bins. It included everything from caramels to butterscotch, from peppermints to gummy worms. Next to the bins was a little metal box with a coin slot. This box was clearly labeled, "Ten Cents Per Sample."

No one ever manned this candy. The sample bins were on the honor system.

I often saw the people I was with put a penny or a nickel in the metal box before helping themselves to a piece of candy. Once, someone put in a token from Peter Piper Pizza while another put in a gum wrapper. I even saw someone put in a piece of gerbil food. Then, they each took some samples.

When I saw this, I laughed right along with them. Then I told them that I'd only put in a penny, when I'd really put in a dime.

Sometimes, I'd even put in a quarter or two to make up the difference. On a few occasions, I returned to this supermarket later in the day and added part of my allowance to the metal box, supplementing for the amounts that were missing.

Every time candy was unfairly taken, I was sure we'd be caught. I'd walk out of the store expecting the manager to tackle us at the automatic doors. He'd take us upstairs to his office and suffocate us with silence and the smell of expired milk. We'd have to sit there until we confessed.

Obviously, I could have solved this obsession by simply not going shopping. But, most eleven and twelve-year-olds don't have that kind of conviction. Besides, I liked hanging out with my friends, and it was only candy. Had anyone asked me to help them bury a body in the jungle gym sand, I would have definitely said no.

A few years later, I had a friend who took thievery to the next level. This girl lived a street over from us. Her name was Karen, but we called her "Kleppie." It was short for kleptomaniac.

Kleppie was a year younger than me and I typically only saw her during winter and summer breaks. She sometimes came over to our house to play and my sisters and I would literally have to keep an eye on the fine china.

Kleppie started stealing out of the blue. One second she was a normal girl reading fashion magazines and trying on makeup. The next she was showing off her bags of loot.

She always stole something different. A tube of lipstick one day, a VHS tape the next. Sometimes she'd steal something small, like a pair of earrings, only to follow it up with something large, like a red bulky sweater.

To this day, I have no idea how Kleppie managed to steal so many things without getting caught. After her reputation was known, I refused to be in the same store with her.

To Kleppie's credit, she was quite generous with her thievery. She was always giving away her stolen items, like a misdirected Robin Hood. Sometimes, I was the unwitting beneficiary.

On one particular afternoon, Kleppie came over to my house and handed me a plastic bag. Inside was a Wilson Phillips tape. I told her I knew it was stolen, and I didn't want it. She promised she had paid for it and acted so upset by my accusations that I actually felt bad not accepting her gift. Finally I told her just to put it in my room.

After she left, I found the tape on top of my dresser. The security sensor was firmly in place and the tape was still in the large plastic crate that tapes used to come in. This tape, with Target price tags, was also in a plastic bag from Osco Drug. It was obviously stolen.

This realization nearly propelled me into a state of panic. I had no idea what to do.

I thought about giving it back to Kleppie, but it occurred to me that she—not exactly a pillar of honesty—might lie and say I'd been the one who stole it. Word would get around the neighborhood and no one would ever hire me to babysit again.

I even thought about taking it back to Target, sneaking it in under my jacket and returning it to the music section. But, I was worried the security sensor would go off the instant I set foot on the premises. Before I could realize, a news van would show up. Lights would be shined into my eyes, and microphones shoved in my face. The press, lovers of alliteration, would dub me "The Target Tape Tramp."

In the end, I decided to hide the tape in the drawer of my nightstand, behind a stack of books. It remained there for years before I finally threw it into a parking lot dumpster. Even then, I still felt guilty. Every time I opened the drawer of my nightstand or heard Wilson Phillips on the radio, I would cringe and hope that no one was onto me.

Getting in trouble was something I feared all through childhood. But it wasn't just a lingering fear that many children have; it was an obsession.

I'd see a cop car go by and fear it was headed to my house for something I did or did not do. I'd hear reports of crime and wonder if I had unknowingly abetted. I'd analyze my actions to assure they were legal. I wasn't merely afraid of being grounded or yelled at; I was afraid of being imprisoned.

Nowadays, I still have rules, but they are not as rigid as they once were. Some things may still be black and white, but often now there is a gray area, too.

A few years ago this gray appeared.

My friend Jenny had called me and told me she'd accidentally stolen a twelve dollar purse from a department store. She had gone to the checkout counter to pay for several items and completely forgotten about the purse in her hand. She didn't realize she hadn't paid for it until she was halfway home, with her toddler and infant in tow.

Rather than telling her to drive herself and her kids back to the store, explain what had happened, and risk an incredulous manager, I simply told her to take twelve dollars and give it to a charity. Surely, a charity needed it more than a well known department store. This is the gray area I am talking about.

My rules may not be as rigid, but my fear of jail lingers on. Sometimes I worry about sending emails filled with false confessions or posting messages on Facebook filled with admissions to awful crimes I know I did not commit. When this happens, I have to retrace all my steps, check every sent email and every social network posting, assuring myself I have not falsely admitted to something horrendous.

I know in my heart that I've never done nor will ever do anything criminal. But, I also know that misunderstandings happen. And when it comes to OCD, misunderstandings can run rampant.

Even with this, I've managed to stay out of the prison system. Which, of course, is a good thing.

Especially since I look really bad in orange.

CHAPTER 4

Ashes to Ashes

THREE TIMES IN MY LIFE I came close to being involved in a fire. The first time was in high school, the second two were in college.

My junior year of high school someone set the school gym on fire, if I may use the term rather loosely. Instead of dousing the basketball hoops in gasoline and sprinkling kindling on the gymnasium floor like a seasoned pyromaniac, someone simply burned down a section of the wooden bleachers. It was a fire small enough to make even Smokey the Bear roll his eyes. My seventh period teacher casually told us we needed to evacuate. She sounded more annoyed than panicked.

Four years later, there was a fire near my college apartment. Luckily, my neighbors Andrea and Michelle were there to serve as heroes.

Michelle had glanced out the back door and spotted a fire in the field behind our complex, raging between the picnic tables and the tennis courts. She yelled for Andrea, put on her shoes, and together they trudged through the mud and sopping wet grass towards the glow of the inferno.

When they got close enough, they realized their five alarm blaze wasn't exactly a threat to anyone. Rather, it was a barbeque aflame to grill a slab of steak and chicken wings.

Crisis averted, dinner cooked.

My third experience with fire came in the same apartment complex a year later. My friend Keith and I had left his apartment and were headed to dinner. We started walking towards the parking garage when we spotted two children who appeared up to no good. Both looked like cats who had just swallowed canaries.

We asked what they were doing. The younger child shrugged his shoulders and stared at the ground. The older child fidgeted with his fingers and said they were selling magazines. He said this as if he was asking a question, trying to see how much we'd believe. I could almost see the canary feather hanging from his mouth.

As they ran off, we smelled something burning. We went around the corner to find smoke dancing around a nearby pine tree. Then we figured out what the kids were really doing.

They weren't so much *selling* magazines as they were *lighting them on fire*. They had thrown a stack into the window well adjacent to Keith's apartment and ignited them.

This fire was as dinky as they came. I'm sure it looked like a scene from *Backdraft* to the spiders and beetles stuck inside the window well, but to us it looked about as threatening as a Fourth of July sparkler. It took us less than a minute to put it out.

These were the three times in my life that fire crept in, even when done so through the portal of a barbeque. The other times all came about from OCD.

Looking back, I'm a little surprised an obsession with fire didn't begin when I was a toddler. It was during this time that my cousin Travis, a toddler himself, fell backwards into a living room fireplace.

He was in his home in Oregon when this happened. Our great grandfather tried to grab him, but his ninety-four-year-old reflexes were not quick enough and Travis fell into the flames.

Travis ended up being fine. Today, the only remaining sign of this accident is a scar on the back of his upper neck. Since he is a veteran of the war in Iraq, everyone just assumes this scar is from shrapnel.

Growing up, my parents often used this incident to warn my sisters and me to stay clear of fires. If we were running near a barbeque or jumping in front of a smoldering fireplace, they would tell us to be careful and remind us about what had happened to our cousin.

I have always imagined my obsessions to be like little demons working inside my brain: they have little faces and bodies and work inside cubicles. Sometimes, a particular demon endorsing a specific obsession will get a promotion. He will be moved to a bigger office, get a little demon secretary, and suddenly have a lot more influence. Fire was one of these.

This demon first truly gained power when one of the homes of our suburb caught on fire and was destroyed completely.

This house was on the corner of a cul-de-sac impossible to ignore. We walked by it on the way to school, we drove by it on the way to the grocery store, we could see it from the ball fields of the park. We saw this house everyday.

When I was in third grade, the house burned down. To my knowledge, no lives were lost in this tragedy. Not even a cat or a dog or a canary perished. But, that didn't lessen its impact; it would forever be cemented in neighborhood lore, known as a place where tragedy happens. The image of charred roof eaves and plywood boards hanging where windows once stood is as vivid to me right now as the day I first saw it.

With this house in such a visible location, everyone in the community knew about it and everyone talked about it. The rumors at my elementary school spread like the fire itself.

Some kids said that the fire started when a cat knocked over a candle with its tail. Some said that an old lady fell asleep while smoking a cigarette. Some said the family left the oven on while traveling to Florida. Some even said a bomb went off inside the kitchen. The kids who said this claimed to have seen it happen, dodging flying glass as the back door blew out.

To this day, I have no idea how the fire actually started; for me, the cause didn't really matter. I had what my mind coveted—a new obsession.

After this, the fear of fire started climbing like ivies up a college chemistry building.

Coincidentally, it was also around this time we began to learn about fire safety in school.

The firefighters from the station up the street came to our class one week to discuss what to do if ever confronted by fire.

They started by explaining the concept of "stop, drop, and roll," telling us what to do immediately if we ever caught on fire. At first, this concept seemed simple enough; I was fairly sure I wouldn't just stand there if aflame. But then the obsessions set it. Soon, I wondered if reason would elude me in my time of need.

I worried about catching on fire and forgetting the stop, drop, and roll instructions. I feared I was more likely to stumble into a puddle of gasoline than to remember what to do.

I was so worried about this that I chanted "stop, drop, and roll" under my breath for days; I wanted it permanently tattooed in my memory. Sometimes, I wrote the words on the palm of my hand, a place I could easily look if flames ever crept up my back. Other times, I wrote the words on my knee, fearing the fire might start at my hands and burn any written reminders.

I endlessly performed this maneuver in my basement, practicing stopping, dropping, and rolling onto the carpet below. I bruised my knees, hurt my elbow, and hit my head on the bookcase, but still I practiced. I practiced with the dedication of an Olympic athlete and by the time I was satisfied, I could have gone for the gold.

During the next lesson, the visiting firemen explained how to determine if a fire was raging on the other side of a door. They told us to feel the doorknob, and to keep the door closed if it was hot.

After learning this, I spent the rest of my elementary school years feeling all kinds of closed doors for fire. I checked everything from library doors to bathroom doors. A few times I checked cupboards.

Sometimes, a door knob absorbing sunlight or reflecting the heat of the room would give off the tiniest hint of warmth and I'd do whatever I could to keep from opening it. I'd kneel down to tie my shoe or act like I was searching for something in my pocket, all the while waiting for an adult to come along. When they did, I'd watch them open the door as intently as a dog watches a rabbit. Then I'd brace myself, half expecting violent flames to emerge and swallow us whole.

A few of the things the firemen taught us I'd already learned, like how to call 9-1-1 and not to cook without a parent's permission. The latter temporarily left me afraid of even buttering a cracker without adult supervision.

Some lessons stood out more than others, leaving ashes smoldering in my mind.

When the firemen informed us that most people in fires died from smoke inhalation, and not the actual fire, I was taken by complete surprise.

For the majority of my childhood, I had horrible asthma and smoke was among the biggest triggers. I'd inhale smoke at restaurants or breathe in the exhaust from a passing semi and feel my lungs tighten. I'd visit my grandma, sit too close to her as she smoked, and spend the next hour wheezing like a punctured set of bagpipes.

Sometimes I'd have an asthma attack and be hospitalized. But, I never died. In my naïve mind, I figured that if I—an asthmatic— could survive smoke, most anyone else could. Fire, it seemed to me, only killed when it burnt people alive, blistering skin and melting hair.

With the firemen correcting me, the fear of smoke emerged. I worried profusely that our basement would catch fire, the smoke floating to the upstairs and killing us before the flames became visible or the heat was noticed.

I'd often go down to the basement to check. I'd pull the string to the overhead light bulb and it would flicker, winking at me like we were both in on a secret mission. I'd smell the air for smoke and fool myself into believing I could see it, its waves and curls distorting the space around our storage closet.

Sometimes, when we barbequed on the back porch, I'd watch my mom flip the hamburger patties and turn the chicken legs. I'd see the smoke rise into her nostrils, and find myself paralyzed with fear that she'd collapse. I'd imagine her dying, right then and there, all because I wanted my hamburger grilled instead of fried. I'd have to look at her, opening and closing my eyes several times, before I was sure she was still alive. Only when she started speaking could I be truly convinced.

Despite all these obsessions with fire, I felt confident fighting it. But, when the firemen taught us that grease fires could not be extinguished with water, I was beside myself.

I remember how this concept perplexed me: *water was fire's natural conqueror, how could grease render it powerless?* I felt a need to warn everyone—adults and teachers—that some fires couldn't be stopped with water. I adamantly wished that Smokey the Bear would divert his attention from forest fires and focus on the dangers of grease fires instead.

Off and on for a few years, I had the fear of walking into my kitchen to find an angry blaze. I imagined the stove burner igniting a paper towel covered in bacon grease. I saw the flames soaring towards the ceiling. Then I imagined myself, in the literal heat of the moment, forgetting what I'd learned and dousing the flames with faucet water. I pictured the flames dancing and mocking, sticking out their tongues in irreverence, as their destruction spread further.

Each time I saw grease in the kitchen—a pan covered in it, a piece of chicken dripping with it, a drop of it fallen to the linoleum below—I had to make sure it wasn't on fire. I'd stare and stare, looking for the slightest hint of flame. The longer I stared, the more on fire it appeared. I'd eventually convince myself it wasn't on fire, only to return two minutes later, certain a flame had been sparked.

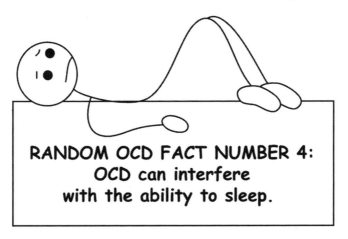

RANDOM OCD FACT NUMBER 4:
OCD can interfere
with the ability to sleep.

These weren't the only things I worried about when it came to fire. I worried that our vehicle would ignite in flames if my mom filled it up with gas while the car radio was on. I worried that a knot in a radio cord would cause an explosion the second I switched the dial to FM. I worried that my grandma would fall asleep while smoking a cigarette. Sometimes, I'd find myself awake at three A.M., checking her blue and white comforter for heat.

Once a year I worried about Santa Claus catching fire as he came down our chimney, landing in a stack of smoldering wood and newspaper.

He'd run into our living room, the flames jumping from his red coat onto our Christmas tree. After unsuccessfully trying to douse the fire with milk and cookies, he'd roll onto the floor, igniting the carpet underneath. Panicking, he'd dash out the front door, leaving a living room engulfed in flames, instead of the presents we'd asked for.

Eventually I got over most of the above, but I didn't let go of my obsession with fire entirely.

By the time I hit adolescence, I felt a bit better about fire. I looked at it as something that could be avoided with the proper precautions. I also looked at it as something that, with smoke detectors, gave a fair amount of warning. But, every once in a while, my obsessions returned.

When I was eleven, we moved from our ranch house to a larger one a neighborhood away. The houses were so close to each other that we didn't even rent a moving van. We moved all of our belongings with my father's pickup.

At our new house, I had a room on the main floor while the rest of the family slept upstairs. I didn't really like this, fearing this meant I'd be the first to be murdered in the event of a break-in. So I slept upstairs whenever one of my sisters was gone for the night. This is where I was on New Years Eve, 1992.

I'd gotten home around one A.M. and crawled into Kim's empty bed. I laid there thinking about the party I'd just attended at my friend Colby's house. The night was dominated by three senior boys who kept threatening to put Colby's dog inside the microwave. I laughed at this notion, but, secretly, I really wanted to call PETA.

Just as I was about to drift off to sleep, I heard a noise outside and got up to investigate. When I looked out the window, I noticed a suspicious vehicle parked in the middle of the road, its engine idling.

I couldn't make out what kind of car it was. It looked like a van, but also like a jeep. Its red brake lights shined in the night, illuminating the mailbox at the foot of our driveway.

I was watching this car intently, furrowing my brows and wondering what it was doing, when a man jumped out from behind the wheel. He grabbed something from the back and ran up to our front porch. He returned to his car empty-handed.

I could never pick this man out of a lineup; his silhouette was all I saw. He had a lean build and long arms. He ran extremely fast. He ran, I told myself, like someone afraid of getting caught.

I watched as he drove his vehicle down the street, stopping a few houses down and performing the exact same act. He didn't seem to follow any kind of blueprint. He simply stopped at a house here, a house there.

I watched him for a few moments until it suddenly occurred to me what he was doing.

Carrying gasoline up to each front porch, this man was dousing the liquid across porch railings and entryway doors right before striking a match. He was leaving the gasoline can behind, hoping the evidence would melt right along with the doorbell.

He was clever. He knew to throw the police off with the lack of a pattern. He chose houses at will, sometimes because they had a basketball hoop and sometimes because they didn't.

As I watched this unfold in my mind, I was paralyzed with indecision. I had no idea what to do.

Part of me knew there were a million things this man could be doing other than committing arson—there had to be a reasonable explanation for his actions. Another part of me felt compelled to check: just walk downstairs, cup my hands on the front window, and lean my head against the glass, searching for a glowing inferno. But, I feared the instant I left my upstairs post the man would turn around, headed back for my house. I wouldn't realize he'd returned until I saw his devious eyes staring back at me from our welcome mat.

I sat in bed for three hours, intently listening for the crackling sound of fire. Several times I got up and walked to the top of the stairs, studying the living room below for the glow of a flame. I stared down at the coffee table, searching for any flames reflecting off of its glass.

Finally I fell asleep, believing that either the man was not really starting fires or that the fire had failed to ignite. The odds of either, I figured, were fifty-fifty.

The next morning, I opened the front door to look outside. Everything seemed normal. Later that morning, I walked my dogs down our street and looked for the charred porches of my neighbors' houses. I didn't find any.

A few months later, I was once again sleeping in Kim's room when the exact same thing happened. But this time, logic prevailed. It took me less than a minute to realize this man was not a homicidal arsonist: he was the milkman delivering our two percent.

Sometime after this, while still in high school, I became obsessed with the stove being left on. At first this obsession was warranted: my father constantly forgot to turn it off.

One of my chores growing up was doing the dishes; I was supposed to do them every night. Often, I left the dishes in the sink, heading to my room and feigning loads of homework. I hoped the dirty dishes would magically disappear. Sometimes, they did.

On occasion, my dad would do the dishes for me. I'd walk into the kitchen and hear the whir of the dishwasher. I'd smell the Comet used to scour the sink. Then I'd turn to leave and notice that the stove burner, previously warming a pan of peas or leftover macaroni, now sat empty. But its red light remained glowing; it was left on high.

I'd tell my dad he left the burner on and he'd just shrug as if it was no big deal. He would have noticed before a fire started.

At first, this didn't really bother me. I wasn't even sure an empty stove burner could ignite a fire. But, once my imagination grabbed hold, I became obsessed.

I'd find myself constantly checking the burner, making sure someone had turned it off and making sure the burner had not turned itself back on. If I was leaving, I'd remind my dad to turn the burner off, the same way a parent reminds a child to lock the door. I constantly worried that he'd forget. I'd come home and find his burnt body molded to the couch while Fox News blared in the background.

Occasionally, I'd hear my dad making popcorn in the skillet after I'd gone to bed. I'd wait for him to finish, then walk into the kitchen, pretending I needed a glass of water. I'd stare and stare at the burner until I was satisfied it was off. I'd go back to bed only to return a few minutes later and check again.

This obsession was at its worst when I was the last to leave the house. In these instances, I found myself stuck between the stove burner and sanity. I'd have to check the burner thirty or forty times, constantly convincing myself it wasn't really off and returning to check, check, and recheck.

Sometimes, I'd leave my house and fear the burner was somehow still on. No matter where I was, I had to go back. Turning onto my street, I'd expect to see flames shooting from my house like a Roman Candle.

Not once did I assume the burner would cause a minor fire in the kitchen, charring the cookie jar and discoloring the dish rag. Instead, I assumed the burner would cause our entire house to burn down. Flames would split up, spreading to the basement and conquering the upstairs. My turtle, stuck in his cage with no way out, would never forgive me.

Sometimes, I believed a fire would hop from the eave of our roof, landing on the neighboring homes until each collapsed like a row of dominos. The papers would compare it to the Great Chicago Fire of 1871.

Whenever this image popped in my head, I marveled at its detail. I could feel my lungs burning as the smoke invaded them. I could see the flames jumping from our pine tree to our porch light and back again. I could feel the heat on my cheekbones.

I only obsessed about the stove burner starting a fire when I was either at home or had recently left. When outside the house, I obsessed about discarded cigarettes that weren't completely extinguished.

I can't say that this obsession controlled my life. It wasn't quite that intense. Instead, it was more like a micromanager I'd once had at work. He'd drop by my cubicle every half hour to make sure I was entering data instead of playing Tetris on the Internet.

Like this micromanager, my obsession reared its head on a constant schedule. I'd have to drop whatever I was doing and attend to it.

I'd see smoldering cigarettes left on sidewalks, and I'd have to step on them until they were out. If I didn't, I feared the remaining sparks would grab onto the pant leg of the next passerby.

I'd see cigarettes idling in café ashtrays and I'd have to douse them with water, fearing they'd lead to a restaurant fire with tragic circumstances.

I'd see someone toss a cigarette out their car window, and I'd have to walk into the street to put it out with my shoe. If I didn't, sparks would jump into the gas tank of the next car that drove by. The car would explode before turning the corner.

I fretted about campfires and barbeques. Often, I'd have to check ten or twenty times to make certain they were out. Once, I burned my hand checking a piece of charcoal for any hint of flame.

Eventually, my fear of fire began to subside and my obsessions diminished. Until a friend's house burned down.

I don't think that many people can say they know someone who lost their house to spontaneous combustion. It's probably not a very common occurrence. But, my senior year of high school, my friend Ruthie's house was engulfed in flames because of this very reason.

The fire started when a rag that had been used to dry a stained deck overheated in an outside garbage can and spontaneously ignited. The fire began next to the garage and then spread throughout Ruthie's home. Her entire house was destroyed. Luckily, everyone was okay. Ruthie's mom once told me that she grabbed as many family photos as she could on her way out the door. I remember thinking how smart she was to grab things that were truly irreplaceable.

Before this, I thought spontaneous combustion was something that didn't really happen. I thought it was one of those things used to scare people into being careful around heat, the way the boogeyman was used to scare children into behaving. After I realized it was a real thing, I imagined fire starting everywhere. My OCD spontaneously combusted as well.

On hot days, I feared everything and anything could spontaneously combust. The leaves that had fallen in the yard, the workbench in the garage, the television sitting in direct sunlight were all at risk. On one particularly scorching day, I worried about my dog: I hosed her down with the kitchen sprayer just to be safe.

By the time I was in my twenties, OCD took the fear of fire up a notch and I began to obsess about starting a fire on purpose. Sometimes I feared purposely leaving the stove on, other times I feared purposely knocking over a candle. I avoided matches and lighters, fearing I would use them to light my roommate's bed on fire or light the bottom of the living room banister. All this led me to check even more.

I'd give myself an extra twenty minutes before leaving the house to check for both accidental and intentional fires. I'd stare and stare, making sure nothing was aflame. I'd make sure everything was off, everything was unplugged and everything was unlit. And then I'd do it again. And then again. Twenty minutes was never long enough.

My obsessions were at their worst when I was watching someone else's house.

I remember a particular occasion in my mid-twenties. My friend Liz had gone out of town and left me to housesit.

One night at Liz's, I lit a lavender candle to mask the smell of the dog food I'd spilled minutes earlier. I made sure to put this candle in a safe place and I reminded myself, over and over, not to forget about it.

I kept this candle burning until six o'clock, when I was to go on a date.

My date came to get me and suggested we go to an Italian place up the street. I agreed, carefully blowing the candle completely out as I grabbed my coat.

We had barely arrived at the restaurant and helped ourselves to breadsticks when I began to fear I'd purposely left the candle lit. I imagined the sparks jumping onto Liz's coffee table, finding an ally in the stack of papers resting there. I pretended to listen to my date talk about his love for podiatry, willing my ears to tune him out and listen for sirens instead.

I worried about Liz's house all through dinner. I was certain we'd return to find the fire department hosing it down, the chief complaining about the irresponsibility of some people. The only solace I could find was the fact that Liz had several fish aquariums: maybe the water would slow down the blaze.

After dinner, my date wanted to go to a movie, but I had to check the house. I told him that I needed to go back to Liz's and get some Advil for my cramps. I knew at the mention of cramps no guy would dare ask any questions.

When we returned to Liz's, there was no fire. There was no flame. There was no tragedy. It was just like the other thousands of times I'd checked: everything was fine.

These days, I am more cautious about fire than the average person, but I'm not sure I'm obsessive. I do feel my OCD wrecking havoc whenever we are leaving the house for an extended time, such as when going on vacation.

When this happens, I have to make sure, five or six times, that everything is unplugged, and turned off. I also have to stare at the stove a little longer than is normal. I have to do this, just to be sure.

But I've let go of some of my fire obsessions completely.

On Christmas Eves, for example, I no longer worry about Santa Claus starting a fire in our living room. In fact, I haven't worried about that in years.

CHAPTER 5

The Dating Game

IN THE FIRST GRADE, I fell in love. His name was Brian Mansen. He had shaggy blond hair, big blue eyes and he could impersonate the siren of a fire truck like the real thing.

Brian was in my class at school and on my t-ball team (we both wanted to be professional t-ball players when we grew up). We started out as friends and quickly became more when he gave me his pudding cup during morning snack time. It was the elementary school version of proposing. This was when I knew it was meant to be.

For months, Brian and I were inseparable. We sat next to each other in class and chased each other around the jungle gym at recess. We held hands and cuddled without ever a worry about each other's cooties. But then, the unthinkable happened: Brian and his family moved to Texas. I was heartbroken. Dating would never be as easy again.

My elementary school love affair aside, it wasn't until high school that I truly began to date. It all started with my first kiss in my parents' basement with a boy named David. He was a lanky Jewish boy with glasses and an Afro: we both fumbled around each other like blind men in a corn maze. It all ended with a boy named BJ.

BJ was funny and just dorky enough to be charming. He carved my initials into his track shoes and once told me he loved me under a park tree during a rainstorm. The only thing that really bothered me about him was his name. I didn't want him to think that having a name like BJ implied he was actually going to be getting any of those.

BJ was what I would consider to be my first real boyfriend. He was the first of many.

After high school and into the first few years of college, I really only had one other boyfriend, a boy named Scott who worked at Radio Shack and once rescued a baby bird from the window well of my parents' house. I just wasn't that interested in dating. Instead, I wanted to be free to hang out with my friends and do whatever. I wanted a "no strings attached" collegiate experience.

It wasn't until the age of twenty-two that I really began to look for someone. Unfortunately, this was also a time in my life when OCD was the puppeteer to my marionette: it completely dictated the way I went about dating.

Like anyone who has dated a lot, I have my share of horror stories—the guy who looked fine inside a darkened club but in the light had (I swear) three nostrils; the boy who took me to a piano bar and proceeded to push the waitress when she accidentally bumped into our table; the guy who inquired about my favorite sexual position three minutes into our date. I don't know if I was shocked more by the question or the revelation that there was actually more than one position.

These were experiences that may have irked a lot of people, not just those of us with a mental condition. But, then there were the ones that bothered me simply because of my OCD.

The first relationship affected by this was with a boy named Calvin. My friend Jenny set us up, declaring that we were meant for each other and nominating herself for maid of honor at our future wedding.

Calvin had tightly-trimmed brown hair and always tucked his shirt into his jeans. He wore glasses that he took off only to rub his eyes, looking like a tired old man whenever he did. He smelled like Old Spice mixed with spearmint gum.

Calvin was a decent man. He was everything that many girls want. He was protective, kind, goofy, and giving. The only problem I had with Calvin involved the Second Amendment: he always carried a gun.

Now, to be fair, Calvin was a cop. But, cop or not, I didn't understand why he needed a gun on him twenty-four hours a day. Colorado hadn't been the Old West for quite some time.

People, they say, are often afraid of things they don't understand. When it came to guns, this was true for me. I had never been around guns and this amplified my fear of the one Calvin carried.

When I was a kid, my father kept a loaded gun in our house, down in the basement inside an old footlocker. My sisters or I sometimes asked him why he had a gun, and he always said he wanted to be able to protect our family in the event of an intruder. This, to me, was hilarious: my father slept in a second story bedroom.

Sometimes, I'd imagine a robber coming into our house, creeping up the stairs only to be greeted by my father. My father, in a voice of reason, would calmly suggest that the robber "hold on" until he could retrieve his pistol from the locked basement. The robber would chuckle, then leave with our Apple II computer.

That was the extent of my experience with guns. I feared guns because I didn't understand them, but that was only part of the problem.

The other part I blame on OCD.

Though my OCD had many faces, the ugliest one was the fear of harming others. Being near a gun compounded this. The most foolproof way to hurt people, it seemed to me, was to shoot them.

This notion made me desperately afraid of guns. I feared that simply seeing Calvin's gun would make me go crazy and I would yank it from its holster and start shooting everything in sight. I feared shooting Calvin in the stomach then heading down the front steps to look for more victims. I was terrified of heading towards a school or playground.

It wasn't only Calvin's gun I was afraid of.

At fairgrounds and sports arenas, I was afraid of grabbing the guns of policemen who were passing by. Once, while attending a carnival, I had the lingering fear of shooting a teenager as he stood in line for a funnel cake. I spent the next five days searching the newspaper to assure myself that didn't happen.

Another time, at a movie theater, an image popped into my head of me grabbing the gun of the security guard and shooting him in the chest. The image was so disturbing and real that I was tempted to search the lobby carpet for drops of blood.

When I later saw the same security guard munching on some Jujubes near the concession stand, I actually felt surprised.

A month later, while spending the night at my parents' house, I was desperately afraid of sleepwalking, finding my father's gun and shooting my parents as they slept. The only way I could sleep was by tying my foot to the leg of my bed with a red rubber jump rope. This, I reasoned, assured I didn't go anywhere.

So, you see, it wasn't just Calvin's gun that scared me. But his gun was the one that was always around.

Calvin often came over to my house with his gun hanging from his belt. I'd go to give him a hug and I'd feel a bulge near my hip (and not even a happy to see you bulge). He'd act dismissive and simply say he forgot to take it off.

To be fair to Calvin, he didn't know I had OCD and a deep dread of grabbing his weapon and opening fire. Had I told him, I think he would have been fine with keeping the gun away from me. But, this was a time in my life when I was very much closeted about my fears. I didn't tell him, not because I was embarrassed, but because I was afraid he would think I actually *wanted* to shoot people. As a cop he would have no choice, my OCD whispered, but to arrest me on the spot.

The longer Calvin and I dated, the larger my obsession with his gun became. We would walk through the park and I'd have an intrusive thought, a vision of myself grabbing the gun and shooting a child as he went down the slide. We'd be watching a Bronco game in my parents' living room and I would fear shooting the children across the street, hanging out the upstairs window like a Lee Harvey Oswald wannabe.

In order to prove my thoughts wrong, I'd have to study the children for gaping holes or exit wounds. I'd watch the child on the slide or those across the street carefully. Only when they giggled or jumped up and down was I certain they weren't mortally wounded.

Sometimes, Calvin's gun wouldn't even be on him, and yet the fears would still appear.

Once, while we were visiting some friends who lived on a street filled with children, Calvin left his gun in the car. This terrified me too. I not only feared this act would end badly, but I was certain. It was my version of death and taxes.

I remember sitting on their blue sofa, anxiously tapping my fingers against the armrest, imagining the kids outside breaking into Calvin's car and getting his gun. I tried to distract myself by listening to what my friends were saying, but I constantly tuned them out until their words just became sounds in the background. I was stuck inside my own head, glued there by terror. I feared it was only a matter of minutes before we heard a shotgun blast and went outside to find a ten-year-old face down in a pool of blood.

After a few minutes, I told Calvin I needed to go to the car to retrieve the lip balm I'd left in the console. I got his keys and went outside. Instead of going near the car, I carefully looked up and down the street, searching for signs of any children.

I could hear far away sounds—the bark of a dog, a truck with a very loud bass—but saw nothing. I repeated this ritual throughout the night, once telling my friends I just wanted to see what the weather was doing, another time asking them to show me their new garden. Each time I really had an ulterior motive: I wanted to be certain there were no children near Calvin's gun.

Another time, at the house of a different friend, Calvin left his gun in his car again. It was again parked in a neighborhood filled with kids. A few minutes after arriving, he told me he had to go back outside; he wasn't sure he'd put the safety on. He may as well have told me he used to be a woman: I couldn't believe what I was hearing.

Ultimately, Calvin and I broke up, not because of his gun but because of other relationship hazards that end so many liaisons. But, the gun, at least for me, was one of the heavier straws on the proverbial camel's back. I wasn't happy to see Calvin go, but I was elated at the thought of never seeing his gun again.

With Calvin out of my life, I wasn't entirely sure how to meet new people.

I didn't want to meet people at the bars, and meeting through work was never a good idea. So, I ultimately looked for an entirely new avenue. I found what I was looking for on the Internet.

I had used the Internet for this very purpose a few years earlier, towards the tail end of college when I came across a dating website while trying to find notes to Shakespeare's *Othello*.

This led to a short-lived courtship with a boy in the military who drove too fast and once tried to seduce me with what he said was confidential Air Force information (I'd seen the same information on the news a year earlier).

I started Internet dating before it was a fad. There were no Match.com or eHarmony commercials spanning the airwaves; few people knew about it and few people did it. It was even free.

For me, Internet dating gave me something that other ways of meeting people didn't provide—it gave me the ability to screen. With every guy listing their occupation, their likes and dislikes, and a little information about themselves, I thought this was ideal.

With my gun phobia steering the path, I stayed away from anyone who was in law enforcement, was a hunter, or listed Charlton Heston among their heroes. But, these certainly weren't the only screening tools I utilized.

As I described earlier in this book, another part of my OCD

*National Institute of Mental Health (NIMH)

involves a fear of AIDS. Thanks to this, I stayed away from anyone who had any homosexual or bisexual qualities.

Any guy who appeared flamboyant, I ignored. A simple mention of skinny jeans or Donna Summer was enough to make me lose interest. Anyone who said they liked to shop or loved shoes, I automatically omitted. I knew I was being hackneyed, but I wanted to be safe, rather than sorry.

Being that I wasn't an idiot, I knew that AIDS was not limited to the homosexual population: straight people could certainly have it too. This led me to screen out anyone who appeared as if they might have slept around or ever used hardcore drugs.

Any guy who mentioned casual sex, posted pictures of himself with several different women, or appeared to be on steroids (and perhaps sharing needles) was eliminated. Anyone who said they liked to party or was far too skinny (and, therefore, my OCD said, an IV drug user) was never contacted. I even avoided anyone who lived in small towns, since I'd once read in a magazine that STDs were more common in rural areas.

It wasn't that I really believed all the guys I bypassed actually had AIDS, it was that they *could* have AIDS. And that is what OCD does. It turns the coulds into likelihoods and, eventually, sure things. It sits down in its recliner, gets out its TV tray, and eats stereotypes for dinner, feeding off even the most ridiculous notions.

When all was said and done, what this left me with was a much smaller pool: my screening took me from an ocean to a puddle. But, I was fine with this. I wanted the water I was swimming in to be free of all my obsessions.

You would think that going about dating in this manner would leave me missing out on a lot of great guys, and you would be correct. You would also think that screening this way would leave me to meet people with whom I had nothing of substance in common. Again, you would be correct.

In fact, all this really did was lead me to meet people who were polar opposites of myself.

The guy who epitomizes all this was a man named Ryan. I was attracted to his Internet profile because he seemed straight-laced, honest, and he was very good looking (you can have OCD and still maintain your shallowness). Most importantly, he had mentioned that he hated guns.

Ryan and I emailed each other a few times before we decided to meet. His emails were nothing special, but he seemed nice. Besides, I knew enough to know you couldn't tell who people really were until you met them face to face.

We met one night at a restaurant in downtown Denver. Our first date was great. We talked about our lives, our families, and what we did for a living. He seemed to get my sense of humor and was extraordinarily polite. He opened doors for me, picked up the check, and called our waitress "Ma'am."

On our second date, we went to a pool hall, drank beers, and played a few games. I wasn't very good at pool. During a game in college I even managed to prematurely sink the eight ball and break my pool cue all in one shot. But, Ryan did something that impressed me: he let me win.

It was a little obvious that he was throwing the game, but that aside, I liked that he wasn't overly competitive, or too proud to lose to a girl. I had once dated a guy who wore a full baseball uniform, complete with metal cleats, to a kickball game. So, this indifference was a welcomed change.

On our third date, Ryan invited me over for dinner. He made grilled chicken with brown sugar and set the table romantically, complete with roses and a bottle of wine. Everything seemed perfect, but this was short-lived.

The first red flag came when I went to use his bathroom and

walked past the den. I looked in—mainly because I'm nosy—and saw a deer head mounted above a bookcase, hanging on the wall, its brown eyes looking down on me in judgment.

When I returned to the table, I asked Ryan about it. He casually said that he was a hunter, something that seemed odd for someone who hated guns. When I pressed him on the issue, he said he hated handguns, but liked rifles.

I thought this was odd, like hating snow but liking frozen rain. Still, I let it go. We continued to talk about our high school experiences, our hobbies, and our favorite episode of *Friends*.

As the night progressed, Ryan steered the conversation in a more serious direction. He no longer wanted to talk about Phoebe Buffay, he wanted to talk about Warren Buffett. After his third glass of wine, Ryan brought up the most taboo subject of them all: politics.

He started off by telling me that he was very conservative. Since I had grown up with a father who routinely tuned the garage radio to Rush Limbaugh, then constantly nodded in agreement, I was not that deterred by Ryan's political stance. I tended to lean to the left, but I was also middle of the road on many issues (I could walk past a tree without wanting to hug it).

Besides, politics were nowhere near a big part of my life. I also didn't believe a difference of political opinion should ever come between people.

But then, Ryan kept talking. He began telling me his views on race.

As soon as this happened, something in Ryan changed. His face became mean, and he got agitated and sweaty. His breaths got short and he fidgeted his hands. For a second, I thought he might be having a stroke.

And then, he began his monologue.

He started off saying that he would never date anyone of another race, saying this with as much conviction as a Sunday preacher. I could almost see him expecting a choir clad in gold robes to rise up in the background.

I wasn't overly shocked by this: I thought it was closed-minded, yet not surprising. But then he dropped a bombshell and told me he would never even be friends with someone from another race.

You know the feeling you get when you're in a good mood only to have something happen to completely deflate it, like arriving at a honey bee farm after a drive through ridiculous traffic, only to realize you have to go back home to get your EpiPen. That is what this felt like. But, Ryan wasn't done.

He went on to say that not only would he never be friends with someone of another race, but he would never be friends with someone who was friends with someone of another race. Upon hearing this, I couldn't help myself and asked matter-of-factly, "Then who are you gonna be friends with? Members of the Klan?"

Our date ended abruptly and we never spoke again. From then on out, I only referred to him as "Racist Ryan" when discussing him with anyone.

Obviously, my dislike for Ryan had little to do with OCD and more to do with not being a white supremacist. But, my point is that after eliminating the majority of available men because of the tiny chance they could have AIDS or be gun zealots, this was the lot I was left with.

Racist Ryan was not the only guy I dated after setting my OCD-imposed limits, he was just the worst of them. Luckily, our entire relationship lasted a matter of days, but that wasn't always the case.

About a year after Ryan, I was "man shopping" on the Internet when I came across a boy named Bill. Bill's profile was pretty run of the mill. He liked movies and music, worked for a corporation, and was looking for his true love. But, his profile also contained the magic words: he regularly donated blood. This meant one thing— he didn't have AIDS. I was instantly ready to have his children.

At first, I really liked Bill. He was funny and he was very social, something important to me at the time. He also preached honesty, claiming he was as truthful as the cherry-chopping George Washington.

Looking back, he was almost too preachy: he preached honesty like a CEO stealing from the company piggy bank preaches business ethics. Soon I found out why—he was a liar, but not *just* a liar, he was nearly pathological.

Initially, his lying manifested in the form of bragging, something I wasn't too keen on anyway. He told me all sorts of things that ended up being false: he was a star on his college basketball team; he'd gotten a perfect score on his LSATs; he had a Mickey Mantle baseball card; he once ate an entire tub of potato salad while his school cheered for him inside the cafeteria. The latter one, I was sure, came directly from a movie. It also seemed a pretty futile story to tell. Would eating an entire tub of potato salad impress any woman? No. Well, maybe if it was fat free.

I gave Bill a break at first, believing his lies were a means to impress me rather than a form of malice. Besides, he did have a lot of nice qualities. But, soon, they became more than I could bear.

Bill never lied to me about anything big, at least not that I know of. I don't think he hid an affair or a criminal past. Instead, he began lying about what I can only qualify as the "dumbest things ever."

He would lie about what he ate for dinner or what time he went to bed, things that I was simply asking as a means of conversation. He would tell me he was at work while sitting on his couch playing video games. He would tell me he had a migraine, only to go out drinking five minutes later. And he would embellish everyday stories until they sounded like tall tales. I waited for the day when

Babe the Blue Ox made an appearance. Half the time, I don't even think he knew he was lying.

He was a liar, but he was safe. He donated blood. He didn't own guns. He was most definitely a liar, but he was definitely safe.

This kept our relationship going for much longer than it should have. It finally ended after a month straight of fighting. We broke up in the middle of a snow storm and never talked again.

During this time in my life, not only was I guilty of dating guys I shouldn't have, but I was also guilty of meeting guys, and misjudging them based on fear. To be honest, I was a little paranoid. I felt like Joe McCarthy, only with guns and AIDS and other OCD-driven fears being my Communism.

Looking back, there were several guys whom I gave the boot because I let my intrusive thoughts get the best of me. And not all these thoughts involved AIDS or guns.

One of these was with a guy named Al who drove a Mustang and had a braided beard. He was exceptionally nice and genuinely interested in me. He met me at an Italian restaurant and brilliantly feigned interest when I explained who I was voting for on *American Idol*. But, it wouldn't work out...because I was certain he was a serial killer.

I have no idea why I thought this—perhaps it was the braided beard that threw me off. All I remember is him walking me out of the restaurant after dinner, and watching from a street lamp as I got in my car. And then, out of nowhere, the thought hit: *he was going to follow me home and kill me.* For the next hour, I drove around, making sure to lose my imaginary tail.

There were guys who I stopped dating because they drove too fast (and would inevitably hit a child); guys I stopped dating because they constantly traveled (and would for sure be killed in a plane crash); and guys I stopped dating because their cars weren't good in the snow (which, I knew, would cause a fiery crash that would kill us both).

So, really, when it came down to it, not only did I screen out people who liked guns, people who had guns, people who appeared to do drugs, people with gay tendencies, people who appeared to sleep around, and people who appeared to use steroids, but I screened out almost everyone else too. It's the perfect recipe for one of two outcomes: ending up with the wrong person, or ending up alone.

You see now why dating was at its easiest in the first grade.

Luckily for me, my story has a happy ending, despite many years of a romantic life dictated by OCD.

After giving up on searching simply for men who were my OCD's version of safe, I searched for men who I could genuinely find myself loving. And, with that, I found Andrew, a goofball of a man who laughs at everything, has a heart of gold, and lettered in attendance during high school. He turned out to be the man of my dreams, my soul mate, and my husband.

By the way, Andrew is absolutely obsessed with Lifetime movies and can name just about every soap opera character ever created. So, you see, I really did throw that whole "gay tendencies" thing right out the window.

INTERMISSION

It's Not Always OCD

WHENEVER YOU ARE DEALING WITH OCD, it's easy to use it as a scapegoat, blaming it on all your problems, all of your worries, and all of your life's difficulties. Other people may do this too, assuming you are afraid of this and worried about that only because you have a mental illness. Yet, this is not always the case. A lot of the time, people with OCD have fears and worries that have nothing to do with being obsessive-compulsive—they merely have to do with being alive.

Having said that, I offer you an intermission, a time to stretch your legs, take a break and look at some fears that have nothing to do with mental illness or really anything else.

1. I am afraid of spiders, but only if they are weird looking, large, or strangely colored. Spiders that are double-bodied, white, orange, or oddly long scare the crap out of me. Normal looking small black and brown ones are fine.

2. I have been afraid of quicksand for as long as I can remember. When I was little, I thought that it sucked people down into underground worlds where they were forced to cater to human-sized bugs who spoke only in French. While I don't (really) believe this anymore, I still sometimes fear that I'll unwittingly walk into quicksand while strolling on the beach or at the local reservoir.

3. I am afraid of seeing a murder and having to join the witness protection program. For this reason, and others, I make it a general rule not to hang out with killers.

4. Though I know they don't exist, that doesn't stop me from being afraid of vampires. By mentioning this, hopefully people will tell others that this book is about vampires and its sales will increase dramatically.

5. I have always been afraid of having my plane hijacked. It started when I was eight and my uncle and mom let me watch a movie about a hijacked plane the night before we flew home from Oregon. *Thanks for that, guys.*

6. I am afraid of heights. Whether it's a large building or a step ladder, I don't care to be any taller than I really am.

7. I am very afraid of getting rabies. I don't really care if an animal bites me (though I don't encourage it); my only concern is they aren't rabid when they do.

8. I am terrified of killer bees. I've been waiting for them to arrive from Mexico since the 1980s.

9. For the last few years, I've been afraid of mountain lions, but no other wild animals. I'm not afraid of bears, wolves, coyotes, or any other creatures that could attack me in the wilderness…unless they have rabies.

10. I am afraid of ghosts, especially in other people's houses.

A few years back, I was spending the night at my friends Krissy and Vicky's house when, right before bed, Vicky told me their house was haunted.

Krissy was out of town and I was sleeping in her room. I told Vicky that we should both sleep with our doors open so the ghost wouldn't get us. She balked at this, saying that Krissy's cat Albert would come in and pee in her room. But I pleaded and prevailed. A few hours later, I woke up to Vicky yelling.

For a second, I was sure she'd seen the ghost. But I quickly realized she was yelling about waking up to cat pee all over her bed. Courtesy of Albert.

This list of fears is really nothing more than that: simple fears. Even if I didn't have OCD, I would still have these fears, and many others. Even if I didn't have OCD, I would still owe Vicky a new bedspread.

Having fears and worries doesn't mean you are having issues with mental illness. It simply means you belong in a very special club. It's called "everyone" and it comes with being human.

That concludes our intermission. Please return to your seat.

The lights are starting to dim.

CHAPTER 6

A Bump in the Road

WHEN I WAS FIFTEEN, MY cousin Derrick taught me to drive. But rather than actually letting me behind the wheel, he opted to drive himself and narrate instructions.

He showed me how to put the car into park, how to adjust the mirrors, how to manipulate the gas and brake, how to steer from lane to lane. He essentially reinforced everything I had already learned by playing *Pole Position* at the local arcade.

Towards the end of this outing, Derrick accidentally drove down the wrong side of a street that ran in front of my old elementary school, the cement median separating where we were from where the law stated we should be. The entire lesson would have been perfect, if only we were driving in England.

It was this beginning that should have served as an omen of things to come.

Five long days after I turned sixteen, I went to take my driving test. Possessing every stereotype of the typical DMV worker, the instructor was an old, angry man, who wore a wrinkled brown suit and acted as if his face would actually split in two had he ever tried to smile.

This man succeeded in scaring the shit out of me; I remember being surprised my nervous hands could grasp the leather of the steering wheel and my shaking foot could find the gas. He said very little, only occasionally sniffing or clearing his throat in a condescending tone.

With his beady eyes burning a hole in the gas gauge, and all my high school hopes resting on the dusty dashboard of the DMV's Honda, it's fair to say I choked a bit. I drove a little too slow, broke a little too late, and put my turn signal on after the turn had already been made.

When all was said and done, I sat silently, pulling at the sweaty t-shirt stuck stiffly to my back, waiting for the words I didn't want to hear. To my surprise, those words never came.

Instead, the instructor looked at me the way a doctor looks at a newly-discharged patient too sick to go home and delivered the news: I passed my driving test by a whopping one point. Watch out world, here I came.

Even with this, I turned out to be pretty good behind the wheel. I obeyed the speed limit, I followed traffic laws, I never drove drunk, and the only thing I ever consistently hit was the large white pole in the parking garage of my college apartment, a pole that I swore jumped out in front of me despite being cemented into the asphalt below.

Unfortunately, being a good driver wasn't enough to save me. Not enough at all.

In fact, I could have been the best driver in the world. I could have gotten 100 percent on my driving test. I could have had the smoothest technique, swerving to miss suicidal squirrels and blown tires without losing an ounce of control. I could have been chosen to drive the Popemobile on world tours. I could have even been among the five people in America who actually knew what to do when approaching a flashing yellow light.

I could have never made a mistake. I could have never moved my hands from the ten and two position and still it would have happened. Still, I would have ended up running people over....

At least inside my mind.

Looking back, I realize I have always been conscientious about driving. Long before my cheesy picture graced the front of a Colorado driver's license and long before my feet could even reach the brakes, I was worried somehow something bad just might happen.

When I was little, my father would often place me on his lap and let me steer his pickup while he manned the gas and brakes. I'd find myself wondering if my lack of experience, not to mention my inability to see over the dashboard, would end in tragedy.

I sometimes worried that I'd steer the pickup into the house on the corner, crashing through the dining room just as the family inside sat down for pancakes. Other times I fretted about hitting an innocent bystander: running over my neighbor Tom as he raked leaves in his front yard or the lady across the street as she jogged with her Golden Retriever.

It wasn't just the steering that left me stressed, it was something else. I was one of the only kids in America preoccupied with the notion of drinking and driving.

During the 1980s, campaigns everywhere warned of the dangers of this. Public service announcements filled the television with images of dummies bloodied and bruised, newspapers told horrific stories about teens who went to prom and never came home, and demolished cars crushed in half stood like statues on city fairgrounds, warning people to make responsible choices.

Now, as a child, it's fair to say I wasn't much of a drinker. The one experience I had with alcohol involved my father offering me a sip of his Budweiser at a summer barbeque. I thanked him by gagging and declaring with the worldly confidence of a six-year-old how yucky beer was.

It wasn't the alcohol that worried me, it was something entirely different. Because I interpreted the term "drinking and driving" in the literal sense, I was certain every time my father got behind the wheel with a cup of Pepsi in his console, he was a ticking time bomb.

I remember staring as he poured cola into the glass, the sounds of ice cubes crackling underneath. I wondered how my father, someone whose only crime was occasionally throwing his household trash into construction site dumpsters, could so defiantly drive while drinking a Pepsi.

Sometimes, I imagined us getting pulled over, me doing my best to gulp down the remaining evidence as my father chewed and swallowed the aluminum can, only to complain of heartburn later.

Other times, I'd sit on the picnic table at school, listening while my peers told of the uncle arrested for writing bad checks or the older brother caught sneaking into a Skid Row concert, and I'd think about my own dark family secret: *my father drinks and drives.*

Eventually, I grew to understand that drinking and driving was limited to alcohol: sipping a Pepsi behind the wheel wasn't exactly a reason to turn my father over to the authorities. But, this didn't close the chapter on my anxieties.

The beginning of my actual driving career wasn't marked with obsessions. When I first got my license, I was only worried about three things: sharing a car with my sister, coming up with gas money, and making the '81 Thunderbird we'd inherited from my grandma look like a BMW, or really, *anything* else.

These worries were soon replaced by others.

It came to fruition the winter I turned twenty-one when I went to the local dealership with my mom and college neighbor Andrea. We had high hopes of doing the near impossible: finding a car without finding a car salesman.

I told my mom that I was looking for a Jeep Cherokee. She told me, since she was paying, that I was actually looking for a *used* Jeep Cherokee. And so, the search began.

The only two cars that met this criteria had characteristics I automatically omitted. The first one was white. Since I tended to wash my car about as often as the summer solstice occurred, it was crossed off the list. The second Jeep Cherokee smelled ridiculously of mayonnaise, as if someone had stuffed a BLT between the back seats. If I wanted a car drenched in condiments, I would have been looking for the Oscar Mayer Wienermobile.

After a few hours, the dream of a Jeep Cherokee faded away and I decided on a red Toyota Tacoma. As my mom wrote the check for the down payment, she made it clear that I was to pay her back the second I graduated college, as if I—English degree in hand—would immediately be showered with sign-on bonuses from the thousands of literature firms crowding the metro area.

Before I got this truck, I had always driven cars that were much lower to the ground, a Chevy Corsica, a Saturn, and of course the Thunderbird, a long car the size of a boat that my sister "sank" in an accident outside our high school. Driving a truck was a different experience; it was then when things began to really get bad.

At first I placed the blame solely on my vehicle, pointing a shaking finger at Toyotas everywhere. I reasoned that the height of my truck was making me paranoid: it was so much harder to see over the hood and harder to control than any car I'd ever driven.

I now know that my truck was just the tool upon which OCD hitched a ride—truck or not, it was only a matter of time before I began running over the entire world.

At first I wasn't overly occupied with hitting people. I certainly broke for the child chasing a ball across the street and slowed down in school zones, but I wasn't obsessed with the fear of running over someone. That would come later.

Instead, my obsession was the fear of *causing* an accident.

This all began one evening with the report of a man who caused a fatal crash just north of Colorado Springs. He had abruptly changed lanes, cutting off an unsuspecting car and forcing it to swerve into another lane. As a chain reaction ensued, he drove off, leaving a tangle of cars to suffer the mess he caused.

As horrible as the accident was, it wasn't the accident itself that caught my attention. Instead, it was something the news reported: the driver might not have been aware of what had happened.

The news stated this matter-of-factly, with the female anchor reporting it as nonchalantly as she would the local football scores or the chance of rain. But, to me, there was nothing nonchalant about it.

This was one of those moments when your world freezes, when you look at the clock in the kitchen and swear the second hand has stopped, when you feel as if you've unleashed a pack of dogs you'll never be able to catch. The instant these words came out of her mouth, I knew I'd look at driving in a different light.

Almost immediately, I began to fear that I, too, would cause an accident without realizing it. Soon, my driving habits began to change drastically.

Prior to this, the pet peeves I had while behind the wheel were similar to those of many others. I'd get annoyed by the car who drove too close to my bumper, or the bicyclist who mistook herself for a Ford Focus, insisting on pedaling fifteen miles an hour in the center lane.

I'd get aggravated by the driver who wouldn't wave when I let him in, and freaked out by the one who waved so much I feared she'd pull over and ask me to a Saturday matinee.

I got enraged by the hasty, speeding driver who caused an accident and blamed it on his car. These type of people reminded me of the baseball player who strikes out, only to glare angrily at his bat, as if it somehow is at fault.

Once I realized that I could actually *cause* a crash and never even know, these pet peeves disappeared, deflating like the balloon you let go of before tying shut.

This created a turning point in my life. Before I knew it, driving obsessions were burrowed in my brain like cockroaches: sneaky, lingering, and forever multiplying.

This was the beginning of something awful.

Depending on where I was driving, my obsessions were sometimes more manageable. Driving through neighborhoods and city streets, for instance, usually left me free of the fear of causing a horrific crash. These areas had lower speed limits, typically maxing out at forty miles an hour, and I reasoned that any accident I caused would be too minor to do much damage. My mind didn't have time for fender benders or twenty-five mile an hour sideswipes, it was booked up worrying about fatalities.

I became paranoid about the highway. With so many cars driving at high speeds, I was certain the highway would be where I left my mark, in the form of yellow police tape and white chalk outlines.

At first, I avoided the highway as much as possible, opting instead to drive the side streets, waiting at red lights while the highway traffic sailed by. But, during this time, I was commuting quite a bit between Aurora and Boulder, two cities lying forty miles apart. Eventually, I was forced to quite literally put the pedal to the metal down Interstate 25.

With each mile I drove, I was certain accidents were happening all around me, cars were blowing up, tanker trucks were spilling over, and semi-trailers were catching fire like a scene from *Die Hard.*

Even when I drove with extra caution, sometimes only going forty-five on the freeway, subjecting myself to glares, stares, honks, and enough flips of the bird to make up a flock, I was certain I was going to cause a catastrophe.

This led me to do one of two things. If I was able to, I'd go back and check. I'd take an exit, only to turn around, and return to the scene of the imaginary crime. Sometimes this worked, other times I was sure my act of turning around caused *another* accident. Either way, I couldn't win.

If I wasn't able to go back and check, if I had someone else in the car or if I was running late for my kinesiology final, I would simply continue on, only to spend hours the next day scouring the Internet and newspaper for reports of a fatal accident.

Checking for news reports was always the most time consuming: my mind could not be 100 percent sure that my fear wasn't realized, not even when the lack of a printed article should have silenced it.

Sometimes I'd read an article about an accident in Holly or Salida, places I had never driven through, and I'd convince myself that my eyes were playing tricks on me—instead of Salida, the article surely said Boulder. This would cause me to read, and reread, often reading slowly and aloud, carefully running my fingers under each word like a first grader just gaining a knack for literacy.

By far, the biggest thing I was worried about was changing lanes the same time as someone else. I often wondered how more accidents didn't occur when the person in the right lane and the person in the left lane decided to merge into the center lane at the same time and place. I soon began changing lanes as little as possible.

I worried that every merge, every step on the brake, every push of the gas would cause a massive wreck. I was certain that one day I'd look in my rearview mirror and see behind me a sixty car pileup. The hurt would be laying outside open car doors and across deployed air bags, the unharmed would be staring at me, hands on their hips, shaking their heads in repulsion.

Before long, these obsessions mutated and soon I wasn't only worried about causing an accident, I was also worried that I would do nothing to prevent an accident.

Whenever you drive down a highway, it's safe to say you'll always find a slug of debris: a piece of plastic, a discarded banana peel, a lone shoe that leaves you wondering where the other one is. Typically, this debris is either too small to be an obstacle, or resting on the shoulder, out of the direct line of traffic.

But, sometimes, the debris is hard to miss, both literally and figuratively.

I often worried something on the road, a hubcap, a canvas tarp, a beer bottle, would cause a driver to swerve, sail over an embankment, and fatally crash. Sometimes my mind would have them hit a tree, or plow into a river. Sometimes they'd soar into a building, other times they'd run into a family headed to a dance recital.

Once, I made the mistake of driving from Aurora to Boulder with an old newspaper in the bed of my truck. Halfway to Boulder, I remembered the paper and began to worry that it had flown out, landed in the center lane, and caused a fatal accident. I ended up pulling over on the side of the highway and checking to see if the newspaper was still where I'd left it. I was so visibly relieved to see it that I'm sure onlookers assumed the truck bed contained a lost cashier's check or a winning lottery ticket.

Whenever I saw debris, I knew I couldn't just dash onto the highway and retrieve it; the fourteen minute mile I ran in eighth grade was definitely not going to do me any favors. So, I solved the issue by calling the authorities.

I became an expert at mile markers. I knew the State Patrol's number by heart. And I began to spot highway debris with the accuracy of an eagle spotting a fish.

All of this was time consuming. It was draining. It was devastating. Nearly every day I was certain I'd caused an accident, either through my own actions or through my failure to be proactive. I was living in a world of worry and I was certain things couldn't get worse.

I was wrong.

RANDOM OCD FACT NUMBER 6:
OCD often begins in adolescence
or early adulthood.*

If you can say anything nice about OCD, you would have to compliment its creativity. Just when you're working on conquering one demon, another pops up, like the purple gophers in the old *Whac-a-mole* game. The better you get with your large, rubber mallet, the quicker the gophers start coming right back.

Pretty soon I began to obsess over something worse than causing a car crash: I began to worry that I'd hit a pedestrian.

As soon as this new idea took off, I no longer worried about causing accidents. It was as if my brain had the capacity of an airplane bathroom: it could only hold one occupant at a time.

I began to embrace highways with open arms—they were free of walkers, bikers, and joggers. Residential areas, or any area filled with people, became my greatest fear.

---

*National Institute of Mental Health (NIMH)

To make matters worse, I was living in Boulder during this time.

Many outsiders know Boulder for very specific reasons: JonBenet Ramsey, the riots of 1997, the fifth down in the CU versus Missouri football game. But those of us who lived there knew the city on a more intimate level.

We knew that venturing out to the Hill and not finding any hippies was akin to picking up a stepping stone and not finding any insects crawling underneath. We knew Pearl Street was home to some of the oddest street performers in the country, including a man who could completely stuff himself into a box barely bigger than one meant for a pair of boots. And we knew that walkers and bikers always, always assumed the right of way.

Even if this meant just walking right out in front of a moving car.

Driving in Boulder became a nightmare. I was terrified I would hit someone. Sometimes, I'd hit a piece of cardboard, or a soda can, and I'd be certain that I'd just run over a human being.

In a matter of seconds, my mind would take off: the speed bump I hit in front of the Wild Oats Market would become a lawyer, one spending his life fighting for the rights of the homeless. The pothole I ran over outside my apartment would morph into a doctor rushing to the hospital to deliver triplets. The curb I jumped would turn into a group of kids, outside drawing flowers with their sidewalk chalk.

On occasion, I'd hit a bump in the road and my mind would tell me I ran over a black person and I would think, *I'm not only a murderer; I'm a racist too.*

The only way to quiet my mind was to check. I'd drive back to the point of impact and make sure that I hadn't hit anything with a beating heart, with a human soul.

More often than not, I'd have to retrace my steps five or six times just to be sure. Sometimes, I'd have to retrace them twenty or thirty times.

I can remember once driving through my parents' neighborhood for an hour, so intent on making sure I hadn't hit any kids. After my tenth or eleventh time around the block, a lady flagged me down and asked if I was lost. I smiled and said I was fine, too embarrassed to admit that I knew exactly where I was: I had grown up seven houses away.

Idling at stop signs and traffic lights was the worst. I was sure a pedestrian would walk in front of my car the second I resumed driving. This led me to study the road carefully in front of me, sometimes waiting at a stop sign for one or two minutes before I felt comfortable proceeding.

Other times, I'd go through a traffic light and then pull over on the side of the road, turning my head back so I could study the ground I'd just driven over. I was always looking for a body.

Checking didn't quiet all the doubts. Instead, I'd worry that whoever I hit had simply disappeared from my sight. They had crawled into a field, fallen behind a tree, rolled into the gutter. This caused me to check even more, peering down water drains and searching nearby parking lots, looking for the bruised and bloodied.

Sometimes, I'd convince myself that a puddle of rain or a puddle of oil was really blood, blood left from someone I'd run over. I'd stare and stare at the asphalt until the puddle morphed into the picture inside my mind.

This went on for years, with the severity constantly altering. Sometimes driving was bad, other times it was debilitating. Sometimes it fell in the middle, being just pretty awful.

On one level, I knew I was being irrational. This is common with OCD. I'd drive over to my friend Steph's and she would tell me, with her hypochondria shining through, that she was pretty sure she had leukemia. I would tell her that I was pretty sure I just ran over three kids. Then, for a moment, it would be apparent we both were being ridiculous.

But, most times, logic was trumped by fear and driving sessions left me anxious when I stepped behind the wheel.

Places like residential neighborhoods or downtown Denver were insufferable—it'd take me an hour to get a mile, or forty minutes to drive around the block. Sometimes I would have a late reaction: I'd hit a bump in Golden and not start obsessing until I'd driven all the way to Broomfield. Then, I would have to turn around, drive thirty miles back, and check.

As you can probably guess, I was pretty much late for everything. Even if I gave myself a half hour of checking time, I always ended up late to wherever I was headed. The things I needed to check just continued to mount, like a game of Jenga that wouldn't topple.

In the heat of the moment, nothing was more important than checking. My heart would start pounding, my stomach would ache, a stream of sweat would slide down the back of my neck. I'd be on the verge of a panic attack and still I'd check.

I cared that I was late for work. I cared that I was going through several tanks of gas a week. I cared that I was ruining my clothes by getting down on my hands and knees to search my truck's undercarriage for a dead body. But, I cared about nothing as much as I cared about making sure my fears were fiction.

Eventually, my OCD began to morph again and this time it grew even uglier. Pretty soon, I began to fear I would run someone over on purpose.

When I was nine, my grandmother relayed to me something she had read in the paper. She told me about a little girl riding her bike outside of a middle school. This girl had paused at a crosswalk, looked both ways and waited for the approaching car to pass. Instead, the driver stopped and waved her across. As soon as she began to pedal, the driver hit the gas, running her over and killing her instantly.

I'm not sure why my grandmother told me this story. She might have simply been relaying information, or she may have been providing a life lesson: be careful of those willing to wave you right through.

Whatever the reason, this story stayed with me and as a child I never walked in front of a car if my gut instinct told me not to. I just never trusted those who were driving. Now that I was the one behind the wheel, I didn't trust myself.

I worried about purposely veering my truck into the bus bench where a businessman sat shuffling papers, or into a crowd of children as they stood selling lemonade. I feared purposely knocking over a bicyclist out for a ride or ramming into the bay window of a bar during happy hour.

The more I tried to knock these fears from my head, the more they came back. Trying to erase them was like being told not to think about a giant yellow gorilla. Automatically, the giant yellow gorilla is the first thing that comes to mind.

With these obsessions haunting me, checking became even more important and even more exhausting. I continued to check the roads I had been on and read the papers for reports of hit and runs. But I also added in a new ritual: I'd constantly examine the windshield, bumper and hood of my truck, looking for cracks or dents the shape of a person.

Before long, these rituals became as much a part of my daily routine as brushing my teeth or taking a shower. But they became more than just habits; they became necessity.

I knew I'd really never run anyone over, not accidentally and certainly not intentionally, but the tagline of OCD always found a way to rear its ugly head: *what if* was tattooed on my brain.

Some days were better than others. Sometimes I only had to check a few times, for a few bodies. Other times, the process seemed endless. I'd like to say that *once* I drove two hours out of my way to check a parking lot I had been in earlier. But the truth is I didn't do this just once, I did it *all* the time.

After a few years of checking whenever I drove, a hit and run occurred in Thornton, a city north of Denver. The news reported that this hit and run resulted in the death of a motorcyclist. The only information they released was that the suspected vehicle was a maroon truck. My truck matched perfectly.

Although I had not been in the intersection of this hit and run, I had been in Thornton. I worried somehow I had been the perpetrator.

For the next two days, I walked around in a fog, the way someone walks around after the shock of losing a loved one or receiving devastating news. I checked my truck repeatedly for any signs of impact. Paint chips. Dents. Bits of human skin.

Finally, the news reported that the vehicle had been found abandoned behind a Wal-Mart. It turned out the truck wasn't maroon after all. It was orangish-red with flames of fire plastered on the side. The only thing ever plastered on the side of my truck were the words "wash me" finger-painted in dirt.

Naturally, I was relieved, but I was also disgusted that I'd spent the past two days suspecting myself of a crime I could not have committed.

It was then that I finally realized the road to redemption was a road paved with irony: I had to have a head on collision with my fear.

So, I stopped avoiding neighborhoods. I quit refusing to drive inside downtown. I no longer moved from the right lane to the left lane whenever a bicyclist rode on the shoulder and I told myself, Sigmund Freud style, that sometimes a bump in the road is *just* a bump in the road.

The more I faced my fears, the easier driving became.

I'm still not a carefree driver; never again will I have the attitude of my sixteen-year-old self, windows down and Def Leppard on the radio. But that's okay, Def Leppard gets old after a while anyway. *Seriously, just pour the sugar on yourself!*

I'll always drive with caution and I'll even have lapses, going back to check the road for a body or two. I'll occasionally call the State Patrol to report a tarp in the street or a couch cushion that fell from a moving van. I'll even sometimes ask my husband to slow way down if there is a child within fifty feet of our vehicle. But, driving obsessions are no longer driving me crazy.

Instead of constantly wondering if I've killed someone each time I'm out for a drive, I find myself wondering the same things as everyone else: *Why don't British people have accents when they sing? Do dogs ever get insomnia?* And, *How does the shoe horn industry stay in business?*

This experience forever changed the way I look at driving, not only for myself, but for others too.

Rather than honking at the lady who drives too slow or glaring at the girl braking for no apparent reason, rather than yelling at the teenager who sits too long at a stop sign or flipping off the old man who hesitates before proceeding through a green light, I give them the benefit of the doubt.

Because you just never know what they might be going through.

CHAPTER 7

A Talk with God

THE DAY MY GRANDMA DIED, I sat in the backyard, shocked at the trees swaying in the summer breeze like nothing had happened. It amazed me that they, and everything else, could act so normal: shoppers could go into the supermarket buying things like paper towels and bags of potatoes; the smell of burning charcoal could invade the evening air; traffic lights could go from yellow to red and back to green. I didn't want the world to simply act as if nothing had changed. I wanted it to mourn, or at the very least, notice.

My grandma's death wasn't very sudden. There was no car accident at an intersection, no massive coronary while playing bingo, no freak accident at a rodeo. Instead, her death was like an amusement park ride built on the fairgrounds of Hell—one that took passengers' emotions up and down and spun them around until they were left nauseous and shaking.

She had gone into the hospital simply to have her appendix removed. I always wondered if the universe messed up and removed her life instead.

Before my grandma became sick, I had never really talked to God. I'd heard of him, of course, and I pictured him in my head, not as someone with a long white beard flowing in the wind, but instead as someone with bright red hair and a smile so big his eyes had to close just to make room on his face.

My God was always laughing, looking down on the world with the perpetual happiness that only the creator of hope could possess. He was in my head, but still he was a stranger.

In fact, the only time God even entered my life was during occasional trips to Sunday school, trips where I spent most of my time wondering what the adults were doing while the children were stuck inside a classroom.

I always imagined that the good stuff was reserved for them and pictured people like Joseph and Mary serving as keynote speakers, showering the congregation with inspirational stories and free donkey rides, all while the children were subject to nursery rhymes, watered down orange soda, and two—and *only* two—vanilla cookies.

But now, with my grandma lying on a hospital bed, I did something I had never done before: I started to pray.

Before any of this began, it never so much as occurred to me that the world could somehow exist without my grandma in it. She was as integral to my life as a tree to a forest.

Even with her growing sicker, I was certain she'd be out in no time, back to sitting in her Lazy Boy and making sticky rice for Sunday dinners. After all, the appendix was an organ my fifth grade teacher assured me humans could live without. I figured it was like removing a tooth or losing an eyelash. She'd be fine.

The night she took a turn for the worse, my cousin Judi and Aunt Rachel had planned to take my sisters and me to get Happy Meals. We waited in our living room, glancing out the window at each car that passed in hopes it was them. They never arrived, opting instead to stay by my grandma's side. I have equated Happy Meals with unhappiness ever since.

When my mom was still at the hospital late in the evening, I knew it was bad. This is when I got on my knees, and began to pray. I was ten years old, and I was begging God to save my grandma's life.

My grandma wasn't the first in my family to die. I'd lost a grandfather, a great uncle, a few dogs, and, least importantly, a guppy my

sister accidentally dropped down the garbage disposal while cleaning our aquarium (she said she rescued it, I begged to differ).

But, my grandma's death was different for two reasons: I was old
enough to know what was happening and I thought if I didn't pray
hard enough, God wouldn't do what modern medicine couldn't—
he wouldn't save her.

When I first started to pray, I had no idea what I was doing.
I simply began by introducing myself to God and apologizing for
ignoring him all these years. I felt a bit guilty for only coming to
him when I wanted something, but I told myself that I wasn't asking
for a new scooter or the answer to next month's science quiz. I was
only acting on behalf of someone who needed a miracle.

At first, this act brought me a great deal of comfort. I had an
image in my head of my prayer flying up to the sky, like a letter
blowing in the wind. Reaching Heaven, it would be received by an
angel, who'd stamp the word "urgent" on it with red ink; my prayer
would arrive in God's inbox in no time at all.

But, as my grandma became critical, I started to worry that I
was failing her. A voice in my head kept asking, *How can she be
dying from appendicitis?* This wasn't the 1800s. There had to be
another reason.

My grandma's demise was preceded by pneumonia. But, at the
time, I couldn't be 100 percent sure it wasn't somehow my fault. I
wondered if I wasn't praying long enough or clear enough. I worried God wasn't answering my prayers because he wasn't receiving
them. I wondered if I needed to do more.

With these thoughts dancing in my head, I developed a very
detailed prayer and forced myself to recite it each night. I had to
perform the prayer correctly, with hands clasped, head bowed, on
my knees. And I was highly specific in what I was asking: the last
thing I wanted was some kind of misunderstanding.

This prayer was lengthy, taking around fifteen minutes to complete, and I had to say it exactly the same way each night. Any deviation, my brain assured me, might cause God to lose patience, ultimately hanging up on my prayer the way a businessman hangs up on a telemarketer. Afterwards, he'd tell his angel secretary to hold my calls indefinitely and get someone more to the point on the line.

The pressure for this perfect prayer led me to mess up almost nightly: my heart would pound and my hands would shake, getting worse the closer I got to the end. It was like seeing the finish line of a marathon and begging yourself not to trip.

Whenever I did mess up, I had to start over from the very beginning, even if I was nearly done. To keep myself from erring, I uttered the prayer as slowly as possible, cautiously choosing every word. I was like a vegetarian at a steakhouse, carefully studying my choices before ever opening up my mouth.

Sometimes, the prayer would take twenty-five minutes to complete. Sometimes longer. Sometimes, I'd say it correctly and then have a notion that something, anything, just wasn't right. Maybe my mind was wandering, maybe I wasn't sincere enough, maybe I paused too long to collect my thoughts. Whatever the reason, if anything felt wrong, I'd have to do it all again.

Whenever I was interrupted, if my parents called me or my sisters walked in looking for a book to read, I'd end my prayer altogether, waiting until I was alone to start over. This was a conversation between God and me. The angels were already listening; I didn't need my family eavesdropping as well.

I always did this prayer at night, when the only sound I could hear was the TV in the living room or the neighbor across the street working on his car. Night allowed me to concentrate. It also offered me no choice: I knew I couldn't go to sleep until my prayer was done correctly.

My grandma died in the middle of 1988, in the middle of August, in the middle of the night. The phone rang around four a.m. and we all knew it was over.

The next weekend we attended her funeral; I missed her desperately. It was weird, the things I thought while staring at her gold casket.

It floored me that the entire potential of a human life—an immeasurable amount of memories and love—could fit into such a tiny box. I wondered if her casket had any idea the chapter it was closing when its lid slammed shut the final time.

I continued to think about my grandma for months. I thought about the way she looked without her glasses and how her vacuum cleaner had a retractable cord. I thought about the peach tree in her backyard and about the time she tried to unlock the wrong car at the supermarket. I thought about the red lipstick she wore and the picture of John Wayne hanging in her bedroom.

But, even in heartbreak, I told myself that God knew what he was doing.

I'd always believed people died not for reasons like cancer or accidents. These may have been the reasons we saw, but we could only see so far. We were blind to the truth.

Instead, I assumed God had bigger plans. The electrician who died of a heart attack might be needed in Heaven to design halos able to glow in the dark for better night vision. The pilot who died in a plane crash might be needed in Heaven to teach angels how to fly. The comedian who died in a fire might be needed to headline at Heaven's most popular nightclubs.

I figured my grandma was needed for something. Maybe to make her famous spaghetti—the only thing she could really cook—maybe to take care of Heaven's animals, or maybe because the three wise men needed a fourth player for their weekly game of bridge.

Most likely, she was simply needed because my grandfather was tired of existing up there without her.

Whatever the reason, this left me sad, but accepting. I knew I had no choice but to be: she was dead and—baring a magic spell that could bring her back from the dead (something I briefly considered researching)—I could do absolutely nothing about it.

With my grandma gone, I was no longer able to obsess about her dying. So, I began to obsess about something else: I worried about her soul not getting all the way to Heaven, leaving her stuck between our two worlds instead. I imagined her spirit roaming around the living room, stealing sips of coffee and complaining that her death got in the way of watching the new season of *Dallas*.

Before my grandmother's death, I thought I knew exactly what happened when people died. Some people were buried, and some people were cremated. I even secretly wondered if my parents, because of their habit of freezing everything from batteries to cupcakes, would do neither and instead opt to be frozen upon death, placed in the refrigerator between a bag of peas and a carton of rocky road.

These were, of course, just the bodies. The souls went on to Heaven. This I was sure of.

But, with my grandma dead and buried, I started to wonder: *what if they didn't?*

The problem with being religious and having OCD is an underlying, and unrelenting, need to know. OCD didn't merely allow me to take a leap of faith, it wanted me to pop my head into the clouds of Heaven and come back with detailed notes and video footage. OCD wanted an irrefutable documentary of the afterlife with the eloquent voice of Morgan Freeman providing narration.

Of course, being sure wasn't possible.

And so, I began a new routine.

I began praying each night that there was a Heaven and that my grandmother, and everyone else who had ever died, was in fact up there.

Like the prayers before, these had to be specific, exact, and done without any errors. Any mistakes, I told myself, might leave my grandma on the other side of the pearly gates, standing in the freezing rain and looking in on all the fun.

To satisfy myself further, I began checking for Heaven wherever I could.

When I swung on the swings at recess, I'd look up at the clouds and try to see my grandma looking down on me over a flock of geese. Whenever I was on a plane, I'd look out the window for any sign of the afterlife, thinking maybe I'd catch a glimpse of a group of angels standing around the water cooler, gossiping about the alleged behavior of Mary Magdalene.

Sometimes at night, I would beg God to leave something under my pillow—a note, a handprint, a blade of grass—anything that would prove his existence.

About a year after my grandma died, a girl at school began talking about religion. She started telling everyone about Jesus.

This girl was named Brittany. She had bright blonde hair, freckles, and two older brothers—the latter meant she knew everything.

Most of the girls in the sixth grade listened to her intently, always hanging on her every word like a skydiver to a parachute.

Once, Brittany told us if two people wearing braces French kissed, they would end up stuck together. Another time she told us girls could get pregnant from a swimming pool. And then there was the time she taught us exercises that would increase our bust size, something we believed every eleven-year-old should know. But it wasn't until she started talking about Jesus that she gained my undivided attention.

According to her, Jesus was due to come back any day. Convinced that the Son of God's appointment book somehow landed in her hands, I believed her completely.

Brittany explained that Jesus was coming back to handpick those who were worthy of Heaven. Satan, she added, was also coming and choosing those condemned to Hell. On the foreheads of those selected for damnation, Satan would write 666 in permanent ink.

Brittany told us that this was imminent, suggesting we should be less worried about our book reports and more worried about our own salvation. Immediately, the obsessions set in.

A few years prior to Brittany's sermon, I had dressed up as a funny looking devil for Halloween. At the time, I'd felt a little weird about it, like I was making light of evil. Now, certain Satan wasn't one for mockery, I was sure he'd be by to settle the score.

After dedicating an entire afternoon recess listening to Brittany's teachings, I rushed home from school and stood in front of the bathroom mirror. I stood there for several minutes, staring at the top of my head, searching for the tiniest hint of ink. I even grabbed a washcloth, lathered it with soap, and scrubbed my forehead until it was red and burning. I had to be certain no markings existed.

Once I was convinced, I was relieved.

Until, of course, I wasn't.

I didn't really believe that Satan would just stop over, ring the doorbell, and ask my parents if I could come out and play. Rather, I thought he'd hide underneath my bed and leave his mark on my forehead while I slept. Waking up to realize I'd forgotten to do last night's social studies homework would be the least of my worries.

Fueled by this obsession, I began to check under my bed each night, making sure Satan wasn't sitting there with a Sharpie.

This fear also led me to pray.

Suddenly, my prayers consisted of not only asking God to make sure my grandma got to Heaven, but also asking God to keep Satan far away from us all.

As I began to ask for more things, the prayers got more specific, more detailed, and a lot longer. I still had to say them perfectly, and I still could not sleep until I did.

Of all the obsessions I've had, I can honestly say that the one with Satan was the shortest lived. It lasted only a few months and has never returned. Even now, I'm not afraid to openly mock him. *So, the Devil walks into a bar...*

My obsession with praying, and doing it correctly, stuck around for years.

When I was in middle school, I had a pet hamster named TJ. He was yellow with red eyes and annoyingly nocturnal, always running on his metal wheel or attempting an escape from his cage at two a.m. He was the first pet that was just mine; I spent hours taking him for walks on a tiny leash and turning our Fisher Price record player into a hamster carousel.

Whenever TJ saw me, he would move his claws wildly. I used to think he was trying to wave, but I have grown to realize that flipping me off was much more likely (see aforementioned hamster carousel).

One evening, I picked TJ up and noticed that he was bleeding from his nose. That night, I prayed to God, asking him to let TJ be okay. In my prayers, I used that very word: "okay."

The next morning I found TJ dead in his cage. From then on, I was no longer able to use the word "okay" when asking God for something and to this day, I still can't.

Occasionally, I'd catch myself using this word, asking God to let my grandpa be okay or let my mom get to work okay. Whenever this happened, I'd stop as abruptly as a deer in headlights, beg God to disregard my word choice, and start over again. Bit by bit, the prayers got more and more intense.

Three years later, the summer after my freshman year of high school, our dog Taffy died from liver cancer.

She died at home, in our backyard. My mom rushed inside to find something to cover her.

Instead of grabbing a tattered towel or an old bed sheet, she grabbed my baby blanket. Taffy's frail little body was wrapped up in this blanket and buried in our garden, along with her dog dish and favorite squeaky toy.

We all knew that Taffy was dying, so her death was not as hard as it may have been if she'd been hit by a car or succumbed to a sudden illness. To be able to prepare ourselves left me grateful, but there was one thing that annoyed me: my mother's choice of doggy casket. I wanted my baby blanket back.

But, this annoyance was quickly replaced with worry.

The grounds of our garden held many dead animals: birds, hamsters, frogs, the half of a squirrel I found in my neighbor's backyard while mowing her lawn. But, Taffy was the first dog, the first large pet, we'd ever buried there. For a while, I convinced myself that everything grown in the garden was destined to have something wrong with it: the tomatoes might be carcinogenic, the squash could taste funny, the zucchini would most certainly be growing fur.

Gradually, these fears got more ludicrous and I began to fear that Taffy would crawl from the grave, and come into my room for a post death visit. I worried I'd wake up in the middle of the night to see her staring at me from my bedroom doorway. Naturally, her eyes would be glowing and, most likely, she would also have fangs.

Now, I'm certainly not the only person in the world to fear a deceased animal rising from the grave. Anyone who has ever seen

Pet Sematary may have a fear of this (and a fear of having their heel sliced open like a piece of apple). But, I took it to the next level: to me, *Pet Sematary* wasn't a horror movie, it was a true story that simply hadn't happened yet.

And so, yet again, I began to pray.

By this time, I'd been praying for five years. It was a process as detailed and lengthy as ever, and the requests kept adding up. If I failed even once to ask God to protect me from my deceased pet, I knew I would regret it: Taffy would be in my room in no time at all.

I feared Taffy's reincarnation all summer, especially when our new puppy began staring at our garden each night, whining and barking for no obvious reason. Sometimes, I imagined that our puppy could see Taffy in the distance, gesturing that our house was hers. Other times, a gust of wind would blow the flap of our doggy door wide open and I'd imagine that Taffy had just made her entrance.

After a few months of this, I stood back and looked at this fear with rationale.

The weird thing about OCD, or more accurately *one* of the weird things, is its ability to seesaw: on occasion, it allows reason to seep in, like a ray of sun through a broken window shade.

For me, my obsession with Taffy was eventually trumped by logic: I suddenly began seeing the obsession through the mind of someone with the ability to think more clearly.

I started to ask myself what the return of my dog could actually do. Previously, I had wondered if she would enact revenge for all the times I dressed her in my Cabbage Patch clothes and pushed her around in a doll stroller. But, once I really thought about it, I knew she wouldn't do anything at all. I knew if animals could come back to life, it would have been on *60 Minutes* by now or, at the very least, all over the *National Enquirer*.

Still, that didn't keep me from praying. You know, just to be sure.

RANDOM OCD FACT NUMBER 7:
People with OCD often perform
compulsions, types of rituals aimed
at easing their anxiety.

In high school, my praying ritual continued to grow. I would sometimes alter it based on what was going on—if I was flying somewhere, I would beg God not to let my plane crash. When my mom was diagnosed with melanoma, I would pray that it wouldn't spread. If I heard a suspicious noise coming from the basement, I would pray that it was just the furnace, and not a one-eyed serial killer who escaped from Canada.

During this time, I also added another thing to my ritual: the number 13.

For many people, this number is considered ominous. But, for me, the number 13 was always the number I picked whenever I played soccer. Once, my cousin Quinn asked me why I wore this number, telling me it was bad luck. I replied by telling him that it was bad luck to the *other* team. Proud of my wit, I adopted the number as my good luck charm.

Soon, I began a ritual of having to jump on my bed thirteen times after I prayed. I couldn't jump twelve or fourteen times, it had to be thirteen. If I failed to do exactly this number, I was absolutely certain something bad would happen. I couldn't have been more certain of an impending tragedy if I'd given a child the keys to my car and detailed instructions to the nearest toy factory.

On nights where I didn't come home—I stayed with a friend or was on vacation—I would perform this counting ritual in the bathroom, jumping on the restroom rug instead of a bed.

I performed this ritual through high school up until the summer after graduation. I didn't quit because I was convinced of its irrationality; I quit because of something simple: I broke my bed.

I'd been jumping along one night when—right around count number seven—I felt my bed start to sag underneath my feet. This was followed by a creaking noise and a loud bang, like a pan dropping to the kitchen floor. My bed, screaming out in pain, was suddenly lopsided. It remained that way from then on. If my parents ever noticed, they never said anything to me.

After this, I gave up jumping and replaced it with counting. After praying, I would have to count to thirteen. It wasn't as difficult and resulted in less property damage. But, it still had to be done. If it wasn't, God help us all.

It was in college when my obsession with God and praying went up another level, and began to interfere with my life dramatically. It all really began with pot.

Before I got to college, I'd always been afraid to smoke marijuana. If the University of Colorado knew this beforehand, I wonder if I would have been granted admission so easily.

It wasn't so much that I was heeding all the after school specials or the commercials that showed a doper's brain turn into a scrambled egg. Instead, I was afraid of pot because I had a heart defect and was worried that one hit would send me into cardiac arrest. I'd land in Heaven only to have God tell me I should have taken Nancy Reagan's "Just Say No" campaign a little more seriously.

I knew, rationally, that this wasn't true: shooting up heroin might kill me, but pot wasn't nearly as dangerous. Still, I didn't want to take any chances. So, I did something I thought would always keep me from drugs: I swore to God I'd never smoke.

I got through my freshman year and most of the next year without ever trying pot. But, in April of my sophomore year, I found myself at a party with friends who had gone to my high school. We were drinking beer and sitting around the living room when someone brought out a pipe.

By now, I didn't fear pot anymore. In fact, I assumed that healthwise, smoking marijuana was comparable to drinking alcohol, something I was doing quite a bit of in college. So, when someone passed me the pipe, I took a couple hits.

Nothing bad came from this. I didn't hallucinate, I didn't go crazy, my heart didn't jump out of my chest and start break dancing to a Michael Jackson song. In fact, the only odd thing I remember was wanting to change the name of my friend's iguana. I wanted to call him "Foot." All and all, it was a typical night in almost any college town in America.

People call pot the gateway drug for its tendency to lead to harder, more lethal drugs. But, for me, it was a gateway to something else.

I was fine smoking pot. I did it on occasion, but well below the standards of Boulder. I didn't find it addicting or, really, even that powerful. I was never tempted to try other narcotics. In fact, pot didn't affect me much at all. Until the night I remembered my promise to God.

The second I realized I'd broken my promise, my world froze and an image popped into my head: I saw everyone in Heaven—God, the angels, all of my deceased love ones—looking down with angry brows, hands over gaping mouths, fingers shaking their disappointment from side to side. Even now, years later, the memory of this vision is so vivid I feel as though I could reach into my brain with a giant Q-tip and pull it right out.

Soon, I started to panic that God would retaliate for my broken promise.

I began fearing that everything and anything bad was because of me. I begged God to punish me—and only me—for my broken vow. I didn't realize the fears I was having were one of the greatest punishments I could ever be dealt.

When things happened on a global level—a landslide in the Himalayas, a bombing at an American Embassy, an ice storm in Canada—I didn't really think I was at fault. But, when things happened in close proximity to me—a horrific car crash, a high school football player dying of cardiac arrest, a routine surgery gone terribly wrong—the scamp who'd set up camp in my head kept asking, *What if God did this because you betrayed him?*

People, I believe, have a way of claiming ownership to tragedies that happen near them—they cling on and protect these tragedies with a fierceness of a mother bear protecting a cub. The Columbine tragedy belonged to Coloradans. The World Trade Center attacks belonged to New Yorkers. Hurricane Katrina belonged to the people of New Orleans. Perhaps it is just human nature that makes us empathize more with things that happen near us. Whatever the reason, I was no different: I focused on the accidents, the murders, the natural disasters of Colorado. *What,* I worried and worried, *if they were because of me?*

I spent close to a year worrying, fearing that everything bad could have something to do with my broken promise. I begged—BEGGED—God to come to me and tell me that I was being crazy. I daydreamed of him sitting me down and letting me in on a little secret: even he—the Creator of the Universe—had once smoked pot during the stressful time of the Crusades. I prayed for him to tell me that breaking my promise was forgiven.

Now, for someone who doesn't have OCD, I realize that all the above sounds a little egotistical, as if I am so important that any action of mine would force God to retaliate against an entire state full of innocent people. But, it's key to keep in mind that OCD is based only on bad things and never the good; it is driven by fear, not self importance.

If, for instance, my grandmother had made a full recovery from her appendicitis, I would have never assumed it was because of my prayers. I wouldn't have rushed home to hang her hospital discharge papers up on the refrigerator, telling all those passing by, "Look what I did!"

Rather, OCD focuses on the negative. I didn't think to myself, *My praying will save my grandma.* Instead, I thought, *If I don't pray, my grandma will die for sure.*

If I had never broken a promise to God, and nothing bad happened for years and years, I would not have given myself credit: that's just not how OCD works. But, with the promise broken, I couldn't be convinced every tragedy wasn't my fault.

The part of me driven by OCD was like the pack mule: it was the part that carried the burden. Occasionally, it even forced me to scour the newspapers reporting bad news, looking for any mention of my name and my broken vow.

To say this whole experience was nerve-racking is to say that Fat Man and Little Boy were just firecrackers. To feel responsible for the death or demise of another human being was as bad as it got. And that is just what would be the focal point of the majority of my OCD experiences.

During this whole time, it never occurred to me that there could actually be something wrong with my mind. Even with the fear of AIDS, the fear of fire, the rigid rules, and the praying rituals, it never occurred to me that I could have a mental illness. This is the other side of OCD, the side sitting on the shaded part of the street while the OCD driven by a need to clean and organize basks in the sunlight.

My obsession with God retaliating lasted a little over a year, and then was replaced by other obsessions. It was really the tip of the iceberg. If OCD was cancer, it was about to metastasize.

Nowadays, I don't believe that God retaliates, or ever retaliated, for my broken promise. I mean, God invented the 1960s, he can't be that shocked by a little drug use.

I do, however, believe in God, and have come to accept that it is called faith for a reason: if there was proof—irrefutable video footage of Heaven- the word wouldn't fit.

One thing I haven't quite gotten over is my baby blanket. I still want it back. Whenever I tell my dad this, he says, "You know where we keep the shovel."

CHAPTER 8

The Belly of a Babe

I'VE ALWAYS FOUND IT FUNNY that "people never change" and "people change" are both common sayings. It makes me want to tell whomever is creating these adages to just pick a side and hold strong. But, I guess it really doesn't matter. In reality, it seems that people can't help but change. Even on issues and situations of the least importance, some of our views and thoughts are inevitably altered with time.

Let me explain what I mean.

Years ago, my paternal grandparents had mirrors on their bedroom ceiling. When I was a kid, I thought this was great: I'd spend hours jumping on their bed and laughing at the reflection above my head.

In the present day, my view on this has done a one-eighty. The thought of mirrors above my grandparents' bed has left me disturbed, if not completely grossed out.

I'm sure you've experienced a changing view on an equally trivial matter. Maybe you used to put grape jelly on everything and now can't stand it. Maybe you used to love roller coasters and now get motion sickness. Maybe you used to be afraid of spiders and now raise tarantulas.

If you have OCD, you might have experienced a great deal of these changes, trivial matters that should be no big deal. The only problem is these matters aren't so trivial to you.

Again, allow me to elaborate.

My sophomore year of college, the way I looked at nails changed. This seems like no big deal, doesn't it? It seems like my altering views on pointed pieces of metal should have about as much influence as Bill Clinton giving a speech on fidelity. Even so, these changing views succeeded in leaving my life forever changed. Because that's what OCD is always doing: changing your life by messing with your mind.

Really, my imagination must shoulder some of the blame. As I've mentioned before, imagination seems to create many of the problems that arise with OCD. I suppose it's an unwanted lesson in dichotomy: creativity that is both a gift and a curse.

My mind has always been dominated by imagination, taking up so much space that logic doesn't even have room to stretch its legs.

In my younger years, I used this to my advantage. I could take the most ordinary things—a Mickey Mouse jewelry box, a Christmas ornament, an ash tray—and entertain myself for hours with made up stories and tales. I used creativity in school, creating comic strips and drawing pictures. I even once wrote a letter to American Greetings with a list of new ideas for Care Bears. To this day, I still claim partial credit for the creation of Champ Bear.

My imagination was my ally, until OCD reached its potential. Then it became my nemesis, my very own Benedict Arnold.

You can probably tell, from my previous chapters, that OCD was always able to use bits and fragments of my imagination against me, even before the disease was at its apex. But, it wasn't until my early twenties that OCD and logic truly began their game of Red Rover. OCD was successful in getting the crux of my imagination on its side.

One of the times this happened began like a normal day. I was walking to campus, running late for my literature class. The recollection of this moment is so clear that I even remember what I was thinking about.

Over the weekend, I'd met a girl at a fraternity party and started talking to her in the kitchen. I immediately noticed that she added the words "honestly" and "honest" to every fifth or sixth statement.

She'd say things like, "I honestly can't believe how hot it is in here" or "I have to be honest, that was the grossest bathroom I've ever seen." This made me wonder if she was lying every time she didn't preface her statement with a reassurance of sincerity. She had told me she liked my shirt and that it was nice to meet me, both statements void of her truthful prelude.

I was laughing at this notion when I inadvertently kicked a rusty nail laying in the middle of the sidewalk. I thought nothing of this and continued walking on.

I walked about forty feet when the game of Red Rover began in my head. Then the image came.

One of the things that makes OCD so hard to defeat is its quickness: it can produce an image in milliseconds. It's like turning on a TV and immediately seeing a set, cast, and plotline. In no time at all, I pictured a toddler consuming the nail, and having it puncture his windpipe.

Before I had time to process this, my brain began adding details until the entire story unraveled in my head: a mom and her son had been out for a morning walk when the boy's nose started to run. As the mom riffled through her purse looking for a tissue, the little boy scooped up the nail and put it in his mouth. The mom didn't notice anything unusual until her son began choking and turning blue.

I knew, from a logical stance, that this probably wouldn't happen. I also knew that it wasn't my responsibility to guard children from all the nails of the world. But I figured I'd go back and pick it up: it'd only take a minute and wouldn't do any harm.

Except it did.

After tossing the nail in the trash, I continued on to class, thinking nothing of my intrusive thought. I made it halfway up Colorado Avenue when I spotted a penny lying in the gutter of the sidewalk. Once again, a choking child popped into my head.

From that day on, all sorts of things became hazards. The broken glass in the middle of the street could shred a child's throat, the bottle cap laying between blades of grass could rip apart intestines, the shards of metal from a broken car bumper could prove fatally appetizing for a curious kid.

For months, I was consumed with picking these things off the ground. My brain told me if I didn't, and a child consumed something deadly, I would be to blame.

I picked up everything from paper clips to pills of Tylenol, from wads of gum to broken light bulbs. I once even searched a park for three hours, looking for a battery I dropped while fiddling with my Walkman. I never did find it. Part of me still wonders if it ended up in the belly of a babe.

This was certainly not my first experience with OCD, but it opened the book to a new chapter and I soon took on the responsibility of the world.

As I've said earlier, this can be taken the wrong way. It may seem as those of us with OCD view ourselves as omnipotent. But, people with OCD don't fancy themselves as heroes, unlimited in power and potential. We don't slip into phone booths, change into tights, and come out with a giant O across our chest. We don't expect, or want, to be lauded.

Instead, we act out our compulsions in secrecy, hiding our bid to save the world from the rational eyes of family and friends. We act out these compulsions because we feel we have to: visions of "what ifs" dance in our heads like sugar plums on Christmas Eve.

We fret and we worry that if we don't act, something awful will happen. It's a responsibility akin to taking out the trash or scooping up dog poop in the backyard in that we never ever wanted it.

As I continued to pick more and more debris up off the ground, my obsessions with responsibility broadened, no longer limiting themselves to things children could swallow. Soon there were threats around every corner.

That's the funny thing about danger: if you look for it, you can find it anywhere. It's like never noticing the incline of a hill, until you are laboriously pedaling up it. This is exactly what I did.

One morning, while out jogging along the Boulder Creek, I spotted an old man trailing behind me. He eventually overtook me (seriously, I run really slow), and I noticed how heavy he was breathing. He sounded like someone gasping for air after being held under water.

I followed behind him for a hundred yards until he turned off in the opposite direction of where I was headed. Then Red Rover started once more.

The logic side of my mind was telling me that he was fine: everyone breathes heavy when they run, that's the point of exercise. The OCD side was telling me the exact opposite: he was going to collapse.

Despite Boulder Creek being constantly populated with runners, my OCD assured me no one would find him until it was too late. I imagined his body being picked apart by vultures, one bird trading another a finger for a piece of pancreas.

I knew this man was not my responsibility. I also knew I really couldn't do much if he did collapse: I didn't have a cell phone and I only knew the basics of CPR. But, none of that mattered when my OCD whispered in my ear that I must continue to check on him. To opt not to, it told me, would be callous and selfish.

I trailed behind this man for several minutes, only turning off when he began jogging along a busy street. Here, I figured, he was safe: if he collapsed, someone would see him.

This event only furthered my obsessions, lengthening the tango OCD and I performed across the dance floor.

Before college, I had been obsessed with danger in only one way: an intruder entering my home. This isn't to say I didn't heed danger in other situations, but I wasn't obsessive about it. Yet when it came to the fear of an intruder, all systems were a go.

When I was in high school, I'd search my family home each night for any hint of intrusion. I'd throw myself up against the front door to make sure it was shut. I'd check to see that it was locked ten or fifteen times. I'd look in closets and under beds for someone who did not belong. I'd even check in places a person couldn't possibly fit, such as underneath a throw rug. Once, while checking our crawl space, I found a discarded beer can and convinced myself that someone was living in our basement. I imagined him coming upstairs when we weren't home to watch TV and use the bathroom, only to run back into the crawl space the second he heard the garage door open.

What began as an obsession to protect everyone I lived with evolved in college to protecting everyone I was around. Then, it took a wild turn.

Eventually, I became obsessed with helping people who weren't there.

The most time-consuming instance of this happened right before my junior year of college. I was driving from Aurora, back to Boulder.

I'd left my parents' house and made my way down Parker Road. As I turned onto the on-ramp, I spotted a shopping cart resting on the shoulder. At first, I thought nothing of this. Kids were always pushing shopping carts to the most obscure places. Once, I even saw one at the bottom of a swimming pool.

I merged onto the highway and continued heading north when my mind began telling me that a child had been inside the shopping cart. I knew I hadn't seen a child: that would have been obvious. But, I did see *something,* some object sitting in the shopping cart's seat. The more I thought about it, the less sure I became that it wasn't a child.

By the time I drove past Westminster, thirty miles from Aurora, I could see this phantom child as plain as day. He was a three-year-old Hispanic boy, with shaggy black hair and worried brown eyes, eyes filled with the glow of oncoming headlights. He wore a pair of blue overalls with a striped grey and red shirt underneath. His knuckles were white as he clutched the shopping cart handle as tight as he could. He was sitting on the side of the road, scared and alone.

I didn't know why this boy was there. I speculated that he was a kidnap victim, abandoned as the perpetrators fled to Wyoming. Or, maybe, he was lost. He'd wandered away from a nearby house and, seeking anything familiar, crawled into a shopping cart, the same kind of cart used by the grocery store his mother patronized.

The reason he was there didn't matter. What mattered was that he could be harmed, maybe even killed, if I didn't intervene.

As I reached Superior, five minutes outside Boulder, I took an exit ramp and turned around inside the parking lot of a movie theater. Then I returned to the highway, retracing my steps.

I headed back to the shopping cart, fearing I was too late. I imagined the little boy hit by a driver who was too busy adjusting the radio to pay attention. Or, maybe, the little boy crawled from the shopping cart and walked onto the highway. The trucker driving a semi would never have had time to stop.

The stronger these thoughts became, the faster I drove. My pulse raced and my pointer fingers nervously tapped against the steering wheel. I listened to the radio without being able to recollect a single song it played.

I exited onto Parker Road and caught a glimpse of the shopping cart across the interstate, sitting in the same spot as before.

I took a left and returned to the highway on-ramp, just as I had an hour earlier.

This time, I drove past the shopping cart slowly, ready to pull over the instant I saw the hint of a person.

Instead of a toddler, my "child" was a pair of discarded phone books slumping in the child seat like paperbacks with broken spines. They looked exactly like they had an hour earlier. They looked nothing like a child.

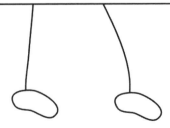

RANDOM OCD FACT NUMBER 8: You can't tell someone has OCD just by looking at them or talking to them.

I didn't find it strange or odd that I'd driven back for a couple of abandoned Yellow Pages. Instead, I found the whole process relieving, and even a little laughable.

It was only months later that I saw this for what it really was: another can opener used to free the worms of OCD.

Following this experience, I started to fear that I'd see children abandoned in a variety of places. Sometimes, I'd worry they would find their way into a crowded intersection, only to be hit by a speeding vehicle. Other times, I fretted they'd come across a pack of matches, and light themselves on fire. I worried they would fall off fences, be attacked by stray dogs, or pull basketball hoops down on top of themselves.

The way I coped with this was to check. Sometimes, I'd keep a watchful eye on neighborhood children until an adult appeared, emerging from underneath a car or walking out the front door of a house. Other times, I'd see a child walking down the street and I'd follow them closely, making sure they got across the road without getting hit. Sometimes, I'd trail behind children as they walked home from school, intent on making sure they arrived at their destination without being harmed. Looking back, more than one child must have thought I was a kidnapper.

Speaking of kidnapping, this was something else my mind grabbed onto, particularly in department stores.

Growing up, I had heard stories of kids snatched from different department stores, only to turn up dead weeks later. These stories convinced me that all kinds of perpetrators went to stores, shopping for five-year-olds instead of toilet paper or shaving cream.

With this fear looming, I found myself completely stressed whenever I saw children alone at a Target or Wal-Mart. The way to cope, once again, was to check.

I'd walk by the toy section and see a four-year-old talking to herself as she grabbed for the Barbies. I'd walk by the magazines and see an eight-year-old smiling as he flipped through a Dr. Seuss book. I'd walk by the food section and see a pair of sisters having a heartfelt debate about Twinkies versus Ding Dongs.

Each time I saw these children, I'd have to wait. I'd walk down the aisle and pretend to be looking at something—a GI Joe doll, *People Magazine,* a pack of powdered donuts—all while studying them through the corner of my eye. I was ready to intervene the instant a stranger appeared with promises of candy or puppies.

I rarely had to wait long. A parent or older sibling was almost always just around the corner, shopping in an adjacent aisle. But, I did have to wait. If I didn't, I feared I would turn on the TV later that night to hear reports of a child abduction. I was physically unable to make myself leave the store until I knew that child was safe.

In a stroke of bad luck, the year I became obsessed with children's safety I was also working at a daycare center.

This daycare center was stereotypical. It was packed with kids and impossible to keep an eye on all of them at once. We tried to keep them entertained with games of football and movies, but they often grew restless.

When the children were bored, some engaged in reckless behavior. They would swing on trees, play with sharp sticks, throw rocks at each other, and climb up on tables the instant any adult turned their back.

Some of them tried to find entertainment in the most dangerous places: I once stopped a six-year-old right as he was inserting a fork into an outlet.

There were two things that made me the most anxious about this daycare center. The first thing was the pool. Since this daycare was part of a recreation center, it had a large one.

I have never been a fan of swimming. Chlorine makes my eyes burn and the elastic strap of goggles hurts my head. Water constantly finds its way up my nose, making me believe I'm drowning when my head's well above pool level. I once even convinced myself, at Celebrity Sports Center, that there was a shark behind me in the water slide: I could not slide down fast enough.

I had never cared for swimming, but when it came to OCD, I downright hated it.

Whenever the daycare kids went to the pool, I was on edge. I'd watch them carefully, bracing myself each time a kid's head went under. I was overly cautious, but not yet obsessive about it. There was a lifeguard on duty and this partly assured me the kids were fine.

Rather, I was most worried about these pools when they were not being used. I worried a child would somehow sneak out of the daycare room, sneak by the front desk, and make his way into the pool. Wanting to look at the bottom, he'd bend over near the edge. Within a few seconds, he'd lose his balance and fall into the deep end. He'd try to swim but without his water wings he'd be helpless. He'd grab for the wall but his heavy clothes would pull him under. He'd struggle for a few minutes until he sank right to the bottom.

This never happened. It never even came close to happening. It would have actually been difficult for a child to get into the pool area unnoticed. But, none of this mattered.

With my OCD holding the reins, I started a routine to assure the safety of all my charges. I'd constantly count the children, making sure everyone thought to be in attendance was actually in attendance. But that wasn't enough.

Sometimes I worried I was counting incorrectly, other times I worried the number I sought was inaccurate: some kids could have arrived without being properly signed in. When the daycare had twins, I worried about counting the same person twice.

In order to truly quiet these worries, I'd take my checking one step further: I'd go and check the pool. I'd tell my coworker I was going to the bathroom and I'd slip into the pool area.

With the smell of chlorine filling my nostrils, I'd walk the perimeter, carefully scanning each end for bodies. Sometimes I'd check while plugging my nose, ready to jump in at a moment's notice.

Often, I'd see something—a pair of dropped goggles, a drain, a diving ring—and I'd convince myself that I was seeing a child, laying motionless at the bottom of the pool. I'd have to stare at the object for several moments before convincing myself otherwise.

I repeated this ritual a minimum of five times a day, but usually more. I wasted hours in that pool, looking for victims who were not there.

The other thing that made me highly anxious about this daycare was the vehicle we used for transportation. It was a red van with a sliding door and two gas tanks.

We used this van to take children to school and pick them up. We also used it to take the kids on field trips to places like Lakeside Amusement Park, the Denver Zoo, and nearby parks.

This van had two seats in the front for adults and several seats in the back for children. Everyone in the van was required to wear seatbelts at all times. The problem, however, was that seatbelts were occasionally breaking, forcing some of the smaller children to share with each other.

I was not allowed to drive the van because I was too young. This always left me sitting in the passenger seat, imagining everything that could go wrong.

My most trying fear was that the kids sharing a seatbelt were not properly harnessed: they could go soaring through the air with every stop we made. I imagined them sailing through the windshield, and ending up on the hood, lying in a bloody mess of glass and windshield wipers. I braced myself every time the driver tapped the brakes.

Sometimes, I'd put my arm up perpendicularly whenever we stopped: inertia, I prayed, was no competition for my six-inch biceps. Maybe my arm could stop them in midair, sparing them the danger of flying head first into a pane of glass. Other times, I'd check the windshield for traces of blood, afraid a child may have sailed through while I wasn't paying attention.

I also worried that some of the older kids would take off their seatbelts while the van was in motion. Trying to impress their friends with childhood defiance, they'd stand up or stick their heads out the window. One would even unlatch the door and jump out onto Chambers Road, mad at me for telling her not to rub her chocolate covered fingers on her shirt.

In order to calm these fears, I constantly watched the children through the side view mirror, and braced my ears for the rebellious sound of a seatbelt unbuckling.

Just as with the pool, nothing bad ever happened in the van. The closest thing we ever came to an accident was hitting a mailbox in the parking lot of the nearest strip mall. All children, and all mailboxes, easily survived.

I wasn't always consumed with these kinds of things: I didn't wake up every single day with them on my mind. This part of my OCD, like all the parts, ebbed and flowed in severity. Some days were awful, other days I only noticed it occasionally. But, it was always there.

Years later, when I was no longer working at the daycare and not really around children, OCD began to outdo itself in terms of originality.

In my late twenties, I moved to downtown Denver to live near my friends John and Steph. While there, I really didn't obsess much about the safety of children. This wasn't because my OCD left, packing its bags and slamming the membranes of my cerebrum shut before storming out.

Instead, I didn't obsess about children because there weren't any around—I could walk the eight blocks to John and Steph's and, most of the time, I wouldn't see anyone under the age of twenty.

The only place in downtown that children frequented was the 16th Street Mall. Even here I wasn't particularly worried: the mall was constantly overcrowded. I assumed there was no way a child could harm himself or get abducted without someone intervening. I was certain that even the local who constantly pretended to be a robot would stop his act and help a child in distress.

On the contrary, I found myself obsessing about other things. I'd walk by a lady who'd been crying and anxiety would set in. Then, like a spool of string attached to a kite, the story would unravel in my mind.

This lady, distraught over a recent breakup, had finally had enough. She'd gone to Walgreens and purchased three bottles of sleeping pills. That night, she'd chase these pills down with a bottle of whiskey, Tchaikovsky's 6th Symphony would quietly play in the background. She'd leave a note that simply read, "Please feed my bullfrog."

I knew that even if this lady was suicidal, it had nothing to do with me: we'd never met. But, the OCD part of my mind oared the boat of guilt and I felt compelled to ask this stranger if she was okay.

Eventually, this obsession morphed into one where I did fear someone would commit suicide as a direct result of me. It had to do with an eighteen cent balance on my Old Navy card.

I'd opened a card a few years earlier for no reason other than I wanted a discount on my Old Navy Performance Fleece. When my bill came, I paid it off completely and cut the card up, knowing I was more likely to lose it than use it.

Unbeknownst to me, I actually hadn't paid the card all the way off: there was still an eighteen cent balance. Because I didn't realize this, I didn't change my address with Old Navy when I relocated.

They eventually tracked me down, looking for their money. But, since my payment was tardy, they had also added a twenty dollar late fee.

I was pissed.

I called them to discuss the situation and ended up speaking to an old man with a heavy Russian accent. This accent, coupled by my phone's lousy reception, frustrated me even more: I couldn't understand what the gentleman was saying.

As he talked, I found myself constantly asking him to repeat what he had said and imploring him to speak louder. We were on the phone for nearly a half hour, over twenty-five minutes spent with misunderstandings.

I finally got my way, and he conceded that Old Navy would retract their late fee. I thanked him and got off the phone.

As I brushed my teeth before bed that night, something about this call began to bother me. And then it hit me: this man would be fired because I'd made it clear that I could not understand him.

I imagined him a Russian immigrant, his parents bringing him over to the states as a baby, intent on fleeing Joseph Stalin's Iron Curtain. I was sure he was near retirement age, with bones brittle and worn: working in a call center was the only job he could do. Then, I imagined Old Navy executives reviewing the tape of our conversation, and determining that he was too hard to understand. They would call him into their office and pull their own Iron Curtain down on his ability to make a living.

I imagined this would devastate him: he'd go home, pull out his

Smith and Wesson, and pull the trigger. He'd die instantly.

As usual, most of me knew this wasn't real. But, my OCD was persistent: it was as if it had formed a picket line, chanting "hell no we won't go" as it held up "it *could* happen" signs in protest. I knew I had to do something.

So, I wrote a letter to Old Navy commending the gentleman I had spoken with. I didn't know his name, but I gave them my account number and knew they could trace it back to the call if they desired. This assured me that he wouldn't be fired, at least not because of anything I had done.

These were just some of the instances I felt the well being of others riding on my shoulders. It happened more frequently than I could recount. To recollect each one would be like counting grains of sand inside a beach pail.

My life was consumed with checking. I checked fanatically, the way children check streetlights for spiraling snowflakes, hoping school will be cancelled. Only I was hoping everyone would be okay.

Like most of my obsessions, this one also changed with time. Nowadays, I still obsess when a child plays too close to traffic or appears lost inside an amusement park, but I don't see danger everywhere I look.

On occasion, I will still trail behind a child in a department store or watch them in their front yard until an adult appears. But, I'm learning that it's not up to me to save the world.

I'm also learning that if my career in writing doesn't take off, I have other options: with years of watching and following under my belt, I'd probably make an excellent stalker.

CHAPTER 9

First Do No Harm

Have you ever had a cramp in the arch of your foot? You might just be sitting there, watching television or reading a book when all of a sudden your foot feels as though it's splitting in half. It comes out of nowhere and the pain is excruciating.

That is what it's like to have OCD with two big exceptions: our pain is emotional and we can't get rid of it by pointing our toes.

I thought I'd experienced this pain before. When I feared I had AIDS or that a stuffed animal was trying to kill my family, I thought this pain was at a climax. When I was certain a child was about to be kidnapped unless I intervened or I convinced myself I was going to jail for a crime I didn't commit, I thought my pain could not get any worse.

I was wrong.

As I have said in the previous chapters of this book, harming obsessions have been my greatest defeat. What began as a concern for others turned into a fear that I would be the one to cause the harm. This was what OCD wanted: this was my foot cramp.

It's ironic, really, that I would end up with harming obsessions.

When I was younger, I had a chance to be really good at soccer. Despite being a slow runner, I was excellent with my feet. I could pass, dribble, shoot, and kick as accurately and far as the best of them. My greatest downfall was that I wasn't aggressive.

"Be aggressive," my coach would yell from the sidelines. "Be aggressive," my mom would say later on in the car. "Be aggressive, be-be aggressive," the school cheerleaders would shout during pep rallies. But, I never was. Even in youth it was always apparent: I am a pacifist.

I should have known OCD would use that against me.

When I started to fear running people over, when I started to fear lighting houses on fire, when I started to fear grabbing the gun of a security guard and shooting someone in the stomach, I should have realized what was building. But, I didn't.

Instead, I figured I could conquer those fears simply by avoiding certain things. I could avoid running people over by not driving my car in pedestrian areas. I could avoid starting fires by not possessing any matches. I could avoid shooting people by staying clear of guns and all those who carried them.

But then OCD found something I couldn't avoid: my own hands.

It's funny how it all works—when you tell someone that your mental illness has reached its boiling point they often think it's because of some big tragedy. They assume you lost a parent to a terminal illness or were sexually assaulted in an airport bathroom. No, I often tell them, it really can be as abrupt as stepping off a curb and being hit by a bus: it can come out of nowhere. At least it did for me.

The day my OCD boiled over, I was doing one of the most stress-free things around: riding my bike inside a park.

That summer, I'd been riding my bike a lot. Not really for exercise but, instead, to avoid driving. Getting behind the wheel had become too time consuming. I kept having to check and check to make sure I hadn't killed someone.

But, if I was riding my bike, I couldn't kill anyone. Or so I thought.

On this day, I was riding down a hill when I stopped at the foot, rolling up the pant leg that kept getting caught in my pedal. Out of the corner of my eye, I saw a girl around the age of ten blowing the white wisps off an old dandelion. I looked at her, remembering how I used to perform that very act, when I suddenly had an image of breaking her neck.

This image came out of an abyss I never knew existed. I didn't plan it and I didn't want it: it was an unwelcome guest in my head.

Just as I'd experienced with other obsessions, this image came on so quickly that I had as much chance of stopping it as a bug does a car grill. The image was also laden with vibrancy, a trait OCD uses to convince the sufferer of authenticity.

At first, I brushed this thought off, knowing it hadn't really happened. But, within a minute, I began to wonder if it had.

I remained on my bike, my hands holding the handlebars and my feet acting like kickstands. For five minutes I stared at this girl, making sure she was moving. At one point, I pedaled near here. I wanted to get close enough to see that she was breathing. The fact that she was standing up wasn't enough to convince me she was still alive. I needed more.

I pedaled up the hill after pulling myself away. I felt like my brain and my obsession were a pair of magnets; pulling them apart required force.

As I reached the top, I looked back down, making sure, once again, I hadn't harmed the child. I only became satisfied when she ran over to her friend and started doing somersaults.

I pedaled home as quickly as I could. It was as if I was trying to out-pedal my OCD, but I couldn't. You can't outrun your own mind.

I passed several people, adults and children, as I rode home. Sometimes I was okay, saying hello or nodding my head as they walked by. Other times, the intrusive thoughts returned.

I'd imagine myself breaking the neck of a man playing catch

or a girl swinging on a tree branch. I literally tried shaking these thoughts from my head, wishing they'd fall out of my ears onto the ground below. But the harder I tried to get rid of them, the stronger they became.

I have no idea how many people I killed on that bike ride home.

Before I go on, let me explain one thing: I have no idea how to break someone's neck. In fact, as far as size goes, I am on the small end. I'm not quick, I'm not trained in martial arts, and I'm not strong.

Instead of actual means, my brain was going off what I'd seen in action flicks—movies where the bad guy grabs someone from behind, and twists their neck in a matter of milliseconds. The victim, slumping over, is dead before they hit the ground.

I believed what I saw in the cinema to be true and was under the impression that breaking someone's neck was as easy as breaking a pretzel in half. Soon, I saw victims everywhere.

A few days after the first intrusive neck-breaking thought, I was running on the track at my old high school. Running beside me, or rather around me, was a huge African American man. His legs were like tree trunks, his buff arms stuffed in his t-shirt like swollen feet into a pair of heels. He looked liked he'd just come from a *Maxim* photo shoot.

I'd been running on the track for a half hour when the image popped inside my head: I imagined myself jumping onto this man's back and breaking his neck. The image came so fast. Neither a confrontation nor a struggle were imagined. Nor was anything realistic: I didn't picture him laughing at my feebleness and flicking me away with his enormous finger. Instead, my OCD convinced me that I was actually a threat to him.

For a few months, I worried about breaking necks everywhere I went. No one was safe in my mind. Children, adults, the elderly, they were all at risk. Arcades. Campus. Grocery stores. It could happen anywhere.

The only way I calmed these fears was to check on my imagined victims. Just as I had done with the girl in the park, I'd stare at my victim for several moments, until they spoke or moved. Until they did something to convince me they had not perished at my hands.

Usually, my thoughts had me killing strangers, but occasionally they focused on people I knew.

I once saw a professor of mine on campus that I didn't exactly adore. I had taken his class, "The Divine Comedy of Dante," merely because I thought it'd be funny (it wasn't) and ended up with a D minus (still passing).

When I saw him walking on campus, the thought of breaking his neck popped into my head and terrified me. I followed behind him for the next twenty minutes, making certain he was not having some sort of late reaction to my assault.

I eventually asked my cousin Derrick, a black belt in Taekwondo, how easy it was to break someone's neck. He told me it wasn't really easy at all—it only looked easy in Hollywood. He also told me it was something that took a lot of strength: I'd never been happier to be a wimp.

This knowledge was what I needed to quiet my neck-breaking obsession, but my other harming obsessions got louder.

The summer before my senior year of college, my friend Beth got married in Denver. At twenty-two, she considered herself a child bride and her marriage didn't stick. Later in life, she married again, this time to her soul mate. I joked around with her, singing "always a bride, never a bridesmaid" whenever I got the chance.

This particular summer saw a first marriage for her and a first for me: it was the first time I ever stabbed anyone.

The morning after Beth's wedding, we'd all gathered in the hotel restaurant for brunch. We sat down to plates full of eggs and hash browns when, all of a sudden, I imagined myself grabbing the knife at my place setting, and stabbing the person sitting next to me.

This person was Rachel, a friend since our freshman year in the dorms. She was certainly not someone I ever wanted to stab. I didn't know why I was thinking these thoughts. But I did know one thing: I needed to check.

I looked at Rachel for any hints of pain. Did she wince as she sipped her orange juice? Was she crying out as she reached for the syrup? Were those tears dripping down her cheeks or just freckles?

I also studied the knife next to me, looking for any hints of blood. The fact that the knife was a butter knife, capable of stabbing margarine but not a person, escaped me.

For several weeks, the fear of stabbing consumed my life. At restaurants and cafes, I constantly worried about grabbing a knife and stabbing the nearest person. When I wasn't eating, I sat on top of my hands to assure this didn't happen.

Eventually, I began to fear stabbing people even when no knives were present.

I remember walking through a department store one evening, looking for Faulkner's *The Sound and the Fury,* when a girl walked right by me, carrying a plastic snowman. All of a sudden, I pictured myself stabbing her, Frosty's frightened eyes glaring at me with every thrust of the knife.

This image was ridiculous: I didn't even have a knife. But, I still had to check. I followed this girl around from aisle to aisle until I was 100 percent certain she wasn't bleeding. Even after I saw that she was fine, I went back to where the image occurred and studied the white floor below, searching for a pool of blood. I was in that department store for two hours and I never bought a thing.

Over time, my OCD let go of the stabbing obsession for one reason: I wasn't as afraid of *hurting* people, as I was of *killing* them. Stabbing, because I had no idea where to aim and I certainly wasn't going to learn, was more likely to result in a painful, but fixable, injury.

My mind, finished with stabbing, moved on to something else.

I didn't seek out these different harming obsessions: it wasn't like I got out a game of Clue and looked for the variety of ways I could off Mrs. Peacock, or anyone else. Instead, it was as if my mind grew another mind of its own and every new harming obsession popped into my head with as little reason and logic as the last.

They also continued to pop in out of nowhere.

I was in Oregon for my uncle's funeral when the next harming obsession appeared. Kim and I were staying with my cousin Quinn in his apartment, while the rest of my family stayed with my aunt.

I was rifling through his refrigerator, looking for a Diet Pepsi, when I suddenly had the image of poisoning his orange juice. At first, I didn't know how I did this: I didn't carry a bottle of arsenic in my overnight bag. But then, I began to worry that I'd used some sort of household cleaner—409, bleach, laundry detergent—and poured it inside the Tropicana.

The intrusive thought lasted a fraction of the time the actual act would take. Poisoning a jug of orange juice, I assume, would take several minutes. I'd have to find something toxic, open it up, unscrew the orange juice, and carefully pour in the poison. But, this was irrelevant: the thought was all I needed to create validity. Even a thought that lasts a millisecond is believable in the mind of someone with OCD.

Before I'd even had time to move a bag of apples and pull out my Diet Pepsi, I was sure the orange juice had been poisoned by my own hand. This proved to be a difficult thing to check: it wasn't as if a skull and cross bones would be floating on top of pulp.

Ultimately, I decided to check by drinking a glass of the orange juice myself. If I didn't become fatally ill, I could rest assured it was lacking in toxicity.

My obsession with poison didn't last long. In fact, it lingered for only a few weeks. It left abruptly, running out of my mind like a scorned lover. I wasn't sure why it had left and I didn't care. I was simply happy to have it gone.

For a while, my mind juggled different harming obsessions. I'd worry about pushing a woman off a bridge one day, and worry about throwing a stroller into traffic the next. I'd worry about attacking an outdoor birthday party with a baseball bat or throwing a child onto a flaming barbeque. Once, on an airplane, I imagined myself throwing a little boy out the emergency door, thirty thousand miles above Illinois.

The next time a stewardess walked by, I searched her face, looking for disgusted eyes staring back at me. I spent weeks thinking this was real and wondering how on earth it didn't make the news.

Of all the harming obsessions I've ever had, there were two that really stuck around. The first was the fear of strangling someone.

My husband Andrew and I constantly watch made-for-TV movies. We sit and poke fun at how easy these types of movies make it look to kill someone. Simply pushing a person down a flight of stairs, for instance, results in death 99 percent of the time. They are, after all, intended to be dramatic.

These movies also make strangling someone look particularly simple. We find ourselves rolling our eyes and shaking our heads every time someone dies after being strangled for five or six seconds. But, part of me isn't amused. Part of me knows that having OCD is like living in a made-for-TV movie: strangulation is as easy as pie.

The day my strangling obsessions began, I was looking for a dog I had noticed on the side of the road. He'd run into a neighborhood and I'd followed in my truck, hoping I'd be able to catch him and reunite him with his owner.

As I was driving down the street, I noticed two little boys around the age of eight playing in their driveway. One of these boys had a cord around his neck; the other boy was attempting to fashion this cord like a necktie.

I specifically remember laughing at this, thinking that these little boys were playing dress up, when the image of me strangling them popped into my head.

Right away, I knew this image was ridiculous: I wasn't capable of strangling anyone. And, besides, I hadn't left my car. But, I decided to turn around anyway and check on the boys.

I returned to the spot where I had seen them, but they were nowhere to be found. Instead of concluding that they had simply gone inside for supper, I was certain that I'd strangled them and tossed their bodies over their backyard fence. One, I imagined, landed on top of a doghouse, while the other landed next to a flattened basketball.

There are some people with my type of OCD who call the police and confess to crimes they didn't commit. These aren't people who want publicity or attention: these are people whose minds have convinced them that they have really committed a crime.

To the rational person, this seems ridiculous: how can you confess to something you didn't do? But, to the OCD suffer, this is par for the course. Obsessive-Compulsive Disorder is so convincing, and so persuasive: if it were a lawyer, it would hardly ever lose a case.

The night I feared I had strangled these boys was the first time in my life I'd ever considered calling the police and turning myself in. That's how bad it got. That's how intense and frightening the image was.

My rational self knew that these images in my head were just that: images in my head. But I couldn't stop myself from wondering, *What if?* If we OCDers were all related, that saying would be on our family crest.

I didn't sleep at all that night. Instead, I watched the news for reports of murders and combed the Internet for any information I could find. I went through the night in a fog, like someone who had been up for three days straight.

The next day, I drove back to their street. The sane part of me expected to see the little boys playing in their yard. The OCD part expected to see yellow police tape surrounding their house.

As soon as I got near their driveway, I saw them: one of the boys was riding his bike, the other was playing inside an open garage. They both stared at me as I drove slowly by, staring back at them. Both kids were alive and well.

I have no idea who these boys are. I don't know their names or whatever became of them. But I do know I will never forget them. I could live to be a hundred and ten and they will still be in my mind, as clear as day.

After this occurred, strangling became my new obsession and it's where I focused all my energy.

At first, I was afraid of strangling both adults and children. I'd see a woman in the ladies room and I'd fear kicking open the stall door and strangling her as she sat on the toilet. I'd be alone with a man in an elevator and I'd imagine grabbing his tie and pulling as hard as I could. I'd load clothes into the dryer of the community laundry room and find my hands tensed, plagued by the fear of strangling the woman next to me with her bathrobe belt.

But, eventually, my fear focused on children. I grew rational enough to realize if I ever tried to strangle an adult (or really harm them in any way) they would totally kick my ass.

I wasn't really afraid of strangling kids with ropes or ligatures. I feared they were so small and helpless that no prop was needed. I was simply afraid of strangling them with my bare hands.

As the remnants of made-for-TV movies danced in the background, I knew strangling a child would only take a matter of seconds.

I'd be walking through the mall, see a little girl near the water fountain, and fear I'd left her strangled. I'd be at a birthday party, see a little boy run by, and the image of myself strangling him as he ate birthday cake would jump in my head. I'd see two middle-schoolers lying in the grass, watching the clouds move over the mountains, and I'd fear they weren't simply *lying* in the grass, they were *dying* in the grass.

The fact that no mass chaos broke out after these images provided no solace. No parents screamed, no men wrestled me to the ground, and no police were called. And, yet, my OCD simply insisted that nobody had seen what I had done.

The only thing that made me feel better was checking. I'd watch closely, waiting for the child to move, to run, to jump, to do anything that verified they were, in fact, alive.

I wasn't afraid of strangling a child calmly and deliberately: I knew I wouldn't just attack a child and begin squeezing out their breath. Instead, I was afraid of going crazy and losing control of my actions. The person doing the strangling would be me, and wouldn't be me.

Once in a moment of desperation, I stood in my kitchen and considered sticking my hand down the garbage disposal as the motor spun. Cutting off my hand seemed to be the best solution: no one ever heard of a one-armed person strangling anyone.

By far, my biggest fear was finding a kid alone somewhere random—a dark alley, a bar bathroom, a pool hall—and losing my proverbial marbles. I'd strangle a child without realizing what I was doing.

This thought made me anxious every time I left my house. I ardently hoped I wouldn't see any children alone and vulnerable. But, one night, I actually did.

My senior year of college, I was walking out of my apartment around midnight, and heading towards the dumpster to throw out our trash. As soon as I turned the corner, I saw a little boy standing on the porch of an adjacent unit.

None of my fears were realized. I didn't go crazy, I didn't lose control, and I certainly didn't have any desire to hurt him. Instead, one question came into my mind, *Why is there a kid out here by himself?*

I knew I couldn't just leave him outside at midnight, so I began walking towards him. I planned to ask him if he needed help, and call the cops if he was lost. The little boy stared back at me, frozen in fear. He didn't move a muscle or blink an eye.

When I got about ten feet from him, I noticed that this little boy was not moving because he was not real: he was a life size cut out of Anakin Skywalker from *Star Wars: Episode 1.*

Nonetheless, I found solace in this moment. I came across what I thought was a vulnerable child and the only thing I tried to do was the right thing: I tried to help him.

My fear of strangling people eventually met a fate similar to my fear of breaking necks: I learned that strangling actually took quite a lot of strength and quite a lot of time. It was nowhere near as easy as it appeared on TV. I was so glad to be a weakling, and an impatient one at that.

RANDOM OCD FACT NUMBER 9:
With the right treatment, people
with OCD can manage their
disease very well.

The other harming obsession that dictated my life was the one
that proved to be the hardest to shake. Appropriately enough, it was
also the most ludicrous. This was the obsession of hanging children.

Hanging was the most ridiculous thing my mind would ever
come up with. The fact that it stuck around just further attests to
OCD's lunacy.

Now, let me say that I have no idea how to hang someone. I
don't know how to tie a noose, I don't know what kind of rope to
use. If there was a class called "Medieval Executions 101," I most
certainly would not take it.

I knew being hanged was not easy. For a few months in college,
my neighbor Amanda and I got into a war of hanging each other's
favorite stuffed animals. We'd hang them from the light in the closet
or the upstairs banister, from the kitchen chandelier or the window
shade. More often than not these animals, weighing hardly two

pounds, wouldn't hold for longer than a few minutes.

But, I wasn't necessarily afraid that *I* would be the one to hang a child, nor was I necessarily afraid that a child would end up hanging themselves. Instead, I was simply afraid of *finding* a child hanging: how he or she got there was not important.

These images started popping up randomly. I'd be doing something as innocent as loading the dishwasher, when the image of a child hanging from the water pipe outside would jump into my mind. Instantly, I'd have to put down the dirty pan, walk outside, and study the pipe for several minutes. I'd feel reassured, but only for a while. By the time I put soap into the dishwasher, my doubts would resurface and, once again, I'd be outside checking.

The stairs outside my college apartment were another trouble spot. I spent hours under them looking for hanging children, checking a foot at a time to make sure I hadn't missed anything. I could physically see that no one was there, and yet, my mind was not convinced.

The parking garage, with cables hanging down and cords all over, was similar torture. It sometimes took me a half hour to go from my parking space to the lot exit, a length of roughly twenty-five yards.

My mind began to see children hanging everywhere.

I'd imagine kids hanging from the rafters of restaurants. I'd picture them hanging from the monkey bars on jungle gyms. I'd convince myself they were hanging from the trees in a park or the eaves of a roof.

It didn't matter if it was physically impossible for a child to be hanging. A tree branch that couldn't support a child's weight or a rafter that was too high for anyone to access were details my mind ignored. Nothing seemed impossible.

I'd try to calm myself by checking, but this made things even worse. The more I checked, the more real the image became.

I'd stare at a basketball hoop, checking to see that no one was hanging from the rim. After staring, after counting, after touching all the parts I could reach, I'd finally walk away, only to return a few minutes later and check again. I had to be sure, but no amount of checking would allow me to be.

Sometimes, I'd place my attention on a particular spot for twenty-five or thirty minutes, looking for any sign of a child. I'd cock my head to the side in complete concentration, the way a dog does when it's really trying to understand what you say.

Areas that I frequented, such as home, work, and local grocery stores, caused me to check the same places day after day, week after week. This checking became part of my schedule and I fit it in daily just as some people do an hour of exercise or a relaxing bath.

If I was leaving work at four, I'd begin checking at three, looking in the bathrooms, the stairwells, the breakrooms, anywhere that needed to be checked. This was something I absolutely had to do before I left, even if it meant that actual work was left sitting in my inbox, untouched. Over time, this ritual became a thing of normalcy; it was as routine as getting a cup of coffee or checking my email.

When things got really difficult, I decided it might be a good idea to keep a journal so I could track my thoughts. This didn't last, as I found it caused me to relive my stress more than it offered help. But, the few weeks I did record can offer insight into the mind of an OCD sufferer, like a step by step guide to being mentally ill. It demonstrates a day in the life with a variety of obsessions. I have retyped a journal entry below:

April 3, 2003

Dear Journal, or whatever. I can't write "Diary" because I'm not thirteen. Today was an okay day, I guess. I left my apartment this morning and had to check the stairs for ten minutes to make sure no kids were hanging. I walked under them a few times and then checked from my car. I could tell no one was there, but my mind kept thinking I had missed something. I was starting to get panicked—and running late for work—so I told myself I had to be done checking by the time I counted to thirteen. I was able to leave, but ended up turning around in the Kohl's parking lot—the thoughts got bad again. The second time, I only checked for about thirty seconds, which to me is a success.

The drive to work was typical. When I got off the highway and onto Havana street, I was afraid I'd hit a man who was waiting for the bus stop. For some reason, this area is always hard for me. I did a U-turn and went back again to check. I drove slow to check for a body. Of course, no one was there. The person behind me honked and glared at me…guess I was driving too slow for them.

I hardly ever fear harming adults anymore, unless I'm in my car. It seems that cars can kill just about anyone. I freaking hate driving. I wish I had a driver. Hell, I wish I didn't have OCD, if we are wishing for things.

Work was okay and I didn't have to check the bathroom before I left, but I did have to check the stairwell four times for any hanging kids. My boss caught me, but I told him I was looking for an earring I had dropped. He offered to help me look, but I told him not to worry about it. He's pretty gullible—a nice quality for any boss.

After leaving work, I stopped at Sweet Tomatoes to get a salad to go. When I was leaving, I was worried that a kid was hanging from the tree outside. I had to sit in my truck until a group of people walked by…I figured if there was a kid, one of them would notice.

I had trouble getting out of the parking lot. I hit a bump by Joe's Crab Shack and was afraid it was a person. I circled around three times before I was satisfied. What do normal people do with their free time?

When I got home the little girl who lives below me was playing outside. I said hi to her and she rolled her eyes at me, which I thought was funny. When I got to the top of the stairs, I looked back at her for a few minutes to make sure I hadn't hurt her. She was playing Jacks (I didn't know kids still did that).

One of my roommates was in his usual mood and greeted me at the door with his typical depression. He always greets me at the door, but always in a bad mood. It's like walking into the world's most depressing Wal-Mart. Every once in a while I get really worried and start fretting over whether he will hurt himself, but I think he's just dramatic.

A few hours ago, I was afraid something had happened to the little girl who was outside playing and I went to check. I checked for about ten minutes, then went back in. I went back to check a few more times, but nothing. It's hard to check at night—it's so freaking dark.

It's eleven o'clock now and I'm trying to get on the Internet. When my roommates and I are all on it at the same time, it is so slow, which makes me want to throw my computer out the window. I heard about a hit and run that happened on Tuesday and I want to get online and make sure it wasn't me. I'm hoping there is a description of the car on the *Denver Post* homepage…usually there is.

For a while, most of my obsessions, including my hanging obsessions, grew much quieter. They weren't totally gone, but they weren't, if you'll forgive me, hanging around as often. But then they returned, and they brought reinforcements.

A few years ago, I started to obsess about things from my past, more often than my present. Instead of worrying that a kid was hanging outside on my pine tree, I feared one had been hanging in my apartment complex in 2005 or from the stairs to my condo in

2003. This made checking hard: I didn't know anyone with a time machine, much less someone who would let me borrow it. But, like OCD, I was creative too.

I implored my husband to call police records and ask if any incidents had occurred regarding ropes and children. I was afraid to do it myself, afraid I'd find myself confessing to hundreds of crimes that never occurred.

I'm not sure how many police departments Andrew called, but it was dozens. He still has the numbers to stations stored in his cell phone.

Not a single person he spoke to had ever heard of any incidents like those I feared, but I wanted to know for certain. I even wanted it in writing, a tangible thing I could look back on for reassurance. Sometimes, I got my wish *(see next page)*.

Today, I still have a variety of harming obsessions: they aren't as bad as they once were, but they aren't gone.

Occasionally, one comes completely out of the blue. Last fall, for example, I feared I had harmed a Girl Scout who came to our door, even though no such girl really existed.

I'd been watching a movie where a child was abducted selling cookies and that was enough to trigger the thought. Soon it snowballed out of control.

I was able to ignore it until later that night, when I went outside to make sure our gate was locked. That's when I saw a trash bag sitting underneath my neighbor's tree.

In what seemed like an instant, OCD had me believing that the Girl Scout was in the trash bag, suffocating from lack of air. I picked up the bag and moved it around, feeling for a human body. I decided it was fine, but that didn't last.

When my husband got home, I told him about my fear, and asked him to check the bag for me. Lifting it wasn't enough, I said,

Serving Our Community Since 1883

May 18, 2010

Andrew Keeler

Dear Mr. Keeler:

Pursuant to RCW 42.56.520, this letter acknowledges receipt of your public records request for a police report regarding any hangings at or near the EWU campus in March 2000 and May or June 2004 (anyone under the age of 18 years) which was received by this office on May 14, 2010.

The City of Cheney has no record for the above referenced information.

Please contact me at ██████████ if you have any questions.

Sincerely,

I wanted him to actually open it and look at the contents. I needed his reassurance.

Obviously, there was no Girl Scout suffocating; it was filled with our neighbor's dog's poop. Andrew really meant it when he said for better or worse.

I know in my heart that harming someone is the last thing I'll ever do, but that doesn't always stop me from checking. Sometimes I risk the long-term disease for short-term peace of mind.

On occasion, I'll just get a feeling that a kid might be hurt in our neighborhood, either on their own or from something I did or didn't do, and I will ask my husband to drive around and make sure everything's okay. When ambulances drive by, sirens blaring and heading in our direction, I'll sometimes follow them, becoming a different kind of ambulance chaser. I know it's ridiculous, but I just have to make sure everything is fine.

Sometimes I wonder if I'm the only person who's ever had these thoughts. But I can't be. Just as I can't be the only person who always assumes, no matter how old I get, that professional athletes are older than me.

In the end, harming obsessions are the most horrific ones I'll ever have. I can't think of anything worse.

And I really hope OCD doesn't take that statement as a dare.

CHAPTER 10

I Know This Sounds Crazy

WHEN I WAS IN SIXTH grade, my sister Kim had a pet gerbil named Oreo. Oreo was, for lack of a better word, a total asshole. He spent his days trying to dig his way out of his glass cage and biting the fingers of any hand brave enough to enter his residence.

One spring, Oreo's tail got infected. It started on the tip and began spreading upwards. Rather than dying prematurely like a good little rodent, Oreo solved the problem by biting his entire tail off. He then went on to live for what seemed like ever.

Some illness is so fixable that even a creature with a brain the size of a pea can find a cure. Other illness is much more complex.

Some people like to believe that mental illness belongs in the first category, that it is laden with simplicity, an ailment with an obvious cure.

They say things like "just don't worry about it" or "mind over matter."

But, for the sufferer, these phrases mean nothing. Saying, "just don't worry about it," to someone who is mentally ill is akin to saying, "just don't wheeze," to an asthmatic.

The term "mind over matter" is equally futile. It might be a nice theory, but when your *mind* is what's the matter, the problem runs much deeper than an old adage can reach.

Mental illness sufferers also must deal with people thinking that it's all in our head. This may be true, but it doesn't make the disease any less real. Having a disease that is all in our head also makes it impossible—short of employing a guillotine—to remove ourselves from the problem.

Stigmas placed on mental illness are factors that lead people to cloak their thoughts in secrecy, ashamed to admit that they need help. But, it's not just the way people look at mental illness that attacks my ailment, it's also the way people look specifically at OCD.

If there is one thing you take away from this book, I hope you learn that OCD is not a disease as cut and dry as people think.

Some people like to say they have OCD because they are irked by a wayward dish in the sink or they feel a compulsion to keep a desk drawer organized. They make a passing joke about how they are "so OCD" because they color coordinate or like things in a certain order.

Yet, those with true OCD are not usually people slightly bothered by an unpleasant thought or a stain on the leg of a pair of jeans.

OCD is not a disease that bothers; it is a disease that tortures.

OCD is also often a hidden disease.

The majority of people with OCD do not go around announcing it. Instead, they wrap it up in old rags and store it in the corner of the garage, hiding it like an alcoholic might hide a bottle of gin.

I know, it might seem weird that I am saying this. I sit here, writing a book on my OCD, while saying it's a disease concealed. But, the reason for my book is not to solicit sympathy or shout, "My name is J.J. Keeler, and I'm Obsessive-Compulsive!" through a loud speaker. My reasons run much deeper.

From this book, I hope people learn how misunderstood OCD can be. It's not always a disease marked by cleanliness or organization. It does not always involve order or germs. Sometimes, people with OCD might even have an untidy room. Sometimes, their only filing system may be found underneath their bed. Sometimes, they might wipe their hands on their sofas in an attempt to clean them.

They may be raging a different kind of battle in their head, one that no one realizes.

I too was once guilty of misunderstanding.

Before I was diagnosed with OCD, I understood it to be the "hand washing disease." And that's really all I thought it was.

It was a conversation with a friend that changed me forever.

At the turn of the century, when everyone was worried about Y2K and the world ending, my friend Danni was worried about a breakup with her boyfriend. This was also the same time I started to have severe OCD. Together, we were a despondent duo, the epitome of misery loving company.

During this time, we went for a lot of walks, walking away from our troubles. It was on one of these walks that we began discussing our biggest fears.

I told her that my biggest fear was hurting others, that I was afraid I would either accidentally or intentionally hurt someone. I told her that I constantly worried about my actions or my inactions causing harm.

Danni, who had once written a college term paper on this very topic, stopped for a moment and said, "It sounds like you have OCD."

I was taken aback by this. I gave her an incredulous smile and said, "I can't have OCD. I hardly ever wash my hands."

It turns out, Danni was right.

After this conversation, I began to research OCD. I surfed the Internet and scoured books at the library. I was surprised to find that the symptoms of OCD were often different than advertised.

I skimmed over the articles about obsessive organization and meticulousness, knowing that—with my wrinkled shorts and holey shoes—those were facets of the disease to which I was seemingly immune. I skipped over passages about hoarding and fanatical washing, knowing that those did not apply.

When I read about OCD sufferers with harming obsessions, I finally took a breath. It was like looking through a microscope into my own life.

What I learned from my research was that a lot of people have this type. It is not just the stereotypical disease it has been branded to be; OCD is a much more complex character.

Over the next few months, I began to read all the material I could find.

The material written by doctors and scientists was helpful, some more than others. But it was the first hand accounts that stayed with me. These accounts had me nodding in agreement and sighing in relief.

Sometimes, I would read something someone with OCD had written and I'd think to myself, *I thought I was the only person in the whole world who ever worried about that.* We OCD sufferers, like all humans, find reassurance in knowing we are not alone.

These first hand stories also proved the most accurate. The reason behind this is simple: those afflicted are often the only ones who can truly understand.

With that, it seems only fitting that I conclude this book by addressing OCD sufferers directly.

CHAPTER 11

Dear Friend,

I am sorry for your struggle. Trust me, I know what you're going through. I am in your shoes. Sometimes I can take them off, but they always seem to find a way back on my feet.

I can't cure you, although I really wish I could. I can't offer a secret potion or a magical recipe. I can't even promise that things will get better. But, I can hope and sometimes that's all we need.

I can also offer you the knowledge I have obtained over the years. Maybe this will help you deal with some of the demons.

In case you are one of those OCDers who happen to like organization, I'll even use bullet points:

- **Understand your obsessions:** The first piece of advice I offer is to understand this disease: understand that thoughts are not real. I know, it's not as simple as it sounds.

  No matter what fear is swirling in your brain, try to remember that obsessions are just that: obsessions.

  According to *Merriam-Webster's Dictionary,* the definition of an obsession is "a persistent disturbing preoccupation with an often unreasonable idea or feeling." Did you notice the word "unreasonable?" How about the word "feeling?" This is all obsessions are composed of: unreasonable feelings. They are not valid, they are not dangerous to others, and they, above all, are not real.

- **Know you are not bad or evil:** It's funny how OCD can screw with the mind, making us believe we are something we're not. We have thoughts and fears that are the antithesis of who we really are. Unfortunately, this is part of the game.

When I started fearing that I was going to run people over with my car or strangle kids in the drugstore, I feared there was a monster inside me, knocking on my soul and wanting out. Maybe you thought this way too.

Those months were the lowest time in my life. Had I known a mental disease was driving this fear, and not a desire to actually harm, things would have been so much easier.

Harming obsessions are devastating, and they can seem very real. They leave me wondering: *what if I act on my thought, what if I snap and hurt someone.* But I know I will never act on them. Neither will you.

You might be wondering how I know this. I have probably never even met you.

But, the fact is, people with harming obsessions don't act on them. They just don't.

I'm sure you want a guarantee. So do I. I want God to come down and give me a certificate saying I will never hurt someone. I want to frame it in gold and hang it above my fireplace.

I can't give you a guarantee, but I can tell you this: people with harming obsessions have these obsessions not because they are bad people. They have them because they are good.

Think about it this way, if you were a killer, or a child abuser, or someone who wanted to harm the elderly, you would not be bothered by these thoughts: instead, you'd find them enjoyable.

Ted Bundy and Jeffrey Dahmer did not sit around worrying that they'd hurt someone. Instead, they fantasized about it, they romanticized it, and they relished in the memories of their victims. We are the complete opposite. OCD is torturing us with harming obsessions because harming others is something we find completely repulsive.

This is OCD's greatest talent. Whatever a person is most bothered by in life—whether it's lack of order, germs, abuse, harm, murder, or blasphemy—OCD will use to its advantage.

Remember that these thoughts are not underlying wants and desires, they are fears. OCD is not us, it's our disease.

Sometimes, with these harming obsessions floating around, it can be so hard to remember that you and I are people of morals, people who are good and right. But, we have to remember this. Tell yourself. Tell yourself right now. I'll wait.

- **Know the power of your mental illness:** Whether you were diagnosed years ago or recently, learn all the traits of your illness. It's easier to cope with when it has the familiarity of an old—albeit unwanted—friend. Still, none of us can expect an instant cure.

  Rationally, I know my thoughts are just thoughts and they are not real. But, as I'm sure you've experienced, OCD is extraordinary talented at replacing rationale with doubt. We have to keep this in mind and understand the power of this disease.

  If you think about it, the human mind is amazing. The human mind put a man on the moon, the human mind invented the automobile, the human mind has advanced medicine so far that people are living decades longer. The human mind is the most powerful thing we have and when it's sick, the power of that illness can be overwhelming.

  Understand this power and know the fight against OCD is not going to be an easy one. Instead, we must arm ourselves with knowledge and all the logic we can muster.

The more I understand my OCD, what sets off my obsessions and what doesn't, what helps to quiet my thoughts and what doesn't, the easier it is to control. This might be the case for you.

- **Ignore what you need to ignore:** Even though I am from Colorado, I am not a skier. In fact, I have been skiing five times in my life. Twice the ski patrol had to rescue me and another time I fell off the ski lift.

  I have no business considering myself a skier just as some people have no business considering themselves experts on mental illness. These are the types of people we need to ignore.

  Being a celebrity or a politician or a person with influence on our society does not suddenly make someone an authority on mental illness. Rather than listening to these people, listen to science, to doctors, to people who have dedicated their lives to studying mental illness, who have passed tests and received degrees in this field, and to those who have experienced it first hand.

  I know how it is. OCD, like all mental illness, can be easy to discard for those who have never had it affect their lives. But it is as real as the sun or the moon.

  A stigma on mental illness remains in our society, but more and more, mental illness is accepted as it should be: a valid, devastating disease.

  As for the people who think it's fake? I'm sure they make you mad. They make me mad too. On a karmic level, it seems only fair that those who believe mental illness to not exist walk in the shoes of the mentally ill, if only for a day. But, I remind myself that people who deny the existence of psychological disorders are quickly being placed in the same category as those who claim to have recently seen Elvis driving a trailer truck through northern Iowa.

- **Accept that it is a life long commitment:** When I was a child, I was stalked by a goat at a petting zoo. This goat was gray and white, with little horns that felt like chicken bones. He immediately took a liking to my cotton shorts and insisted on eating them.

  For half an hour, I tried to avoid this goat. Sometimes I was successful—I lost him at the miniature donkey then cleverly eluded him at the pot belly pig. But, somehow, he always found me. I'd feel a tug on my shorts, only to look down and see him finishing his lunch.

  Unfortunately, this is how OCD works. We may avoid it for a while, but it has a way of finding us.

  For this reason, I've found that it helps to be vigilant. I know that even when OCD seems nowhere to be found, it is still lurking in the dark alleys of my mind. So, I recognize this. I realize that I may always have this disease and I recognize that's okay. *Having* a disease does not mean I have to *succumb* to one.

  It is likely that, more than once, you will get your OCD under control, only to have it return as angry as a customer who found a rat in their food. But, try not to panic. Remember, you evaded the goat before, you can do it again.

- **Know you are not at fault:** OCD is not a disease that anyone seeks out. It is not a disease that anyone deserves. And, it's not a disease anybody wants. It is a disease people just get: it's the hand we are dealt.

  OCD is a biological disease and often genetic (giving us cause, of course, to blame our parents). People should not apologize for having it. People don't need to apologize for having cancer or heart disease or any other type of ailment: mental illness is not an exception.

  It's also important to get on medication if need be. There are many medications available that can and do treat OCD.

If you need help balancing the chemistry of your brain, talk to your doctor about medicine.

- **Find therapy that works for you:** There are different kinds of therapy used to treat OCD. Cognitive behavior therapy is one of the most widely used.

  Not all types of therapy work for everyone. Some might work a lot, some might work a little, and some might leave you wanting to cancel your health insurance in protest. But, remember, there are always other therapies worth a try. If you feel frustrated or stuck in a therapy routine that isn't working, don't be afraid to try a new one. It's your brain and you're free to fix it any way you want.

- **Trust yourself, not your OCD:** OCD is a pathological liar. It sounds so simple, but it's true. OCD wants us to believe the lies it tells—that is its source of power. It wants us to believe that we didn't intervene in a kidnapping or that we broke someone's neck in the restaurant bathroom.

  It's not just in the moment either, OCD can warp memories from years ago. It takes memories and twists them until we are unsure of what's reality and what's not. It's like reading two separate books and then confusing the plots: we find ourselves believing that Hamlet spent his life on the Pequod, tracking down some elusive white whale.

  One of the things so hard to remember is that OCD, in the simplest terms, is full of crap. It's like a poker player without a hand: once we call its bluff, it has no choice but to fold.

  It helps to have a little faith. Whether this is faith in God or the Universe or something entirely different, it helps to have it. Have faith in your treatment, have faith in the truth, and have faith in your healing. More than anything, have faith in yourself.

- **Stop checking:** My parents have a dog named Dudley. He is a chow mix with two great loves in his life: food and walks. I once saw him in the midst of inhaling his dinner when my mom grabbed his leash. I watched as a confused panic took over his face: he looked back and forth between his dish and my mother, not knowing which option to take. It was like *Sophie's Choice,* but for dogs.

  This is what it's like with OCD: we have to make a difficult choice between short-term relief and long-term relief. We can either give into our thoughts and check—make sure that bump in the road wasn't a child or make certain we didn't harm anyone while walking to the library—or we can ignore our thoughts.

  Giving in and checking, as you probably know by now, provides short-term relief; we look and look and eventually see that nothing bad has happened. But, in the long run, checking only gives our thoughts validity and feeds our disease. The more we check, the worse we get. This pleases OCD. If OCD could let out a smug laugh, this is when it would do it.

  I often imagine OCD sitting in its room, sporting a boastful smile and carving a notch in a wooden bedpost each time we check. Sometimes it pats itself on the back or shakes its hands in victory—OCD doesn't just want us to check, it needs us to check: its survival depends on it.

  The other option we have is refusing to check. In the short run, this refusal makes us extremely anxious, momentarily convinced we've caused a tragedy. But, over time, it lessens the power of our obsession and heals our minds. It is the path we must take: no matter how difficult, we must resist the urge to check.

  This won't be painless, and it won't always be successful—I believe there will be instances throughout my life where I will end up checking—but there are a few things that make resisting the urge to check a little easier for me.

First and foremost, I have to decide the second the intrusive thought pops into my head not to buy into OCD's bullshit. Even a second of attention is enough time for the seeds of doubt to be planted.

Secondly, I try to remember that when checking, I am reacting to a thought, not to an action. For instance, if I have the image of throwing my cat into the oven, and then have an urge to open the oven and make sure cat is not really what's for dinner, my need to check is not a reaction to anything real. It is only a reaction to a thought. A thought is just a thought. I tell myself that as often as possible.

Thirdly, I try to control my imagination. The way that I do this is by making my thoughts overly ridiculous. You can see what I mean under the next bullet point, cleverly titled *Make your thoughts overly ridiculous.*

- **Make your thoughts overly ridiculous:** One of the talents of intrusive thoughts is their ability to be virtually unstoppable. The surest way to think about something is to tell yourself not to.

  See for yourself: tell yourself not to think about a purple kangaroo. What's the first thing that comes to mind? I'll bet it's a marsupial the color of grapes.

  It's hard to just bury intrusive thoughts, so I find it helpful to go an extra mile: I make them so unbelievably ridiculous that not even I give them credence. Let me give you an example.

  I'm driving around and I hit a bump in the road. All of a sudden, my mind tells me that I've run over a little kid, maybe a seven-year-old selling Girl Scout cookies. Instead of burying this idea (or buying into it) I perform some alterations: I tell my OCD that I didn't hit just one Girl Scout, I hit an entire troop.

There are arms and legs and Thin Mints scattered all across the road. My windshield is covered with Tagalongs and flying Samoas are pelting my windows. Half the troop lies bloodied in the street while the other half pounds on the hood of my car. A girl with pig tails flips me off. I am shocked by her improper behavior.

Or maybe I'm at a fancy restaurant. I have, to my husband's dismay, just ordered the lobster tail. He turns his head to count the money in his wallet and I spot a steak knife next to his plate. In a flash, I have a vision of grabbing the knife, jumping out of my chair and stabbing the waiter carrying a tray of margaritas. An instant later panic sets in and I think, *Wait, did that really just happen?*

Instead of checking on the waiter or studying the knife for drops of blood, I alter my thought. I tell myself that I did indeed stab the waiter. As the knife went into his chest, the tray of margaritas slipped from his hand. Before I knew it, I was covered in salt and lime. But, I didn't stop there.

I pulled the knife from the folds of his skin and ran over towards the bartender. He tried to fight back, hitting me with a wine bottle and throwing a bowl of peanuts in my direction. But I was too quick. I plunged the knife into his right eye and it came out through his left ear.

Then something weird happened: he broke out in song. He jumped on top of the bar and started singing Cat Steven's "The First Cut is the Deepest." The entire restaurant got up and began dancing the cha-cha.

Sometimes I don't have time to think of such a grand storyline. In these instances, I just alter my thought in simple terms. The kid I imagined strangling at the playground wasn't a kid after all: he was actually a monkey just escaped from the zoo. The toddler I envisioned throwing into traffic was actually a robot. At the point of impact, his head came loose, hanging from red and blue wires. His metal arm dislodged and flew through the air, landing on top of my tennis shoes.

All these scenarios sound over the top, don't they? Well, that's exactly the point. The absurdity is just what makes this tactic successful.

The more absurdities a thought entails, the easier it is to disregard it. And then, all a sudden, the reality that nothing actually happened sets in. Obsessions diminish, and "victims" quickly revert back to what they really were: just intrusive thoughts.

- **Quit analyzing it:** One summer, my husband Andrew and I drove to Oregon for the family Olympics my cousin Derrick hosts every year (and forces us to attend). We left Colorado in the morning and planned to drive to Boise by nightfall.

The years prior to this, my OCD had been greatly controlled—to the point that I hardly noticed it much. But, as we drove to Boise, I could feel something brewing. It was almost like the aura some people get before a migraine.

We made it to Boise safely and rented a room for the night. The next morning, Andrew went to get coffee and fill up our gas tank. I stayed in the hotel getting ready.

I was brushing my teeth over the sink when suddenly an image popped in my head. This image was of a kid hanging by the neck from a jump rope over the hotel balcony. This image came out of nowhere, exploding into my head with sudden and unexpected force, the way a tiny nail can burst the tire of a semi.

Immediately, I found this image ridiculous. The entire time it was in my head, I hadn't moved from the sink. I remained standing there, staring at myself in the mirror, toothpaste foaming in my mouth like a rabid dog.

In fact, the image was so ridiculous that as we left the

hotel, it didn't even occur to me to check the balcony for any hanging children.

But, as we crossed the Oregon border, I made a horrible mistake: I decided to think carefully about the image, believing this action would help me to know it wasn't real.

This plan backfired.

I rolled the image in my head over and over again, imagining more details with each rumination. And things suddenly began to get much worse, spiraling out of control like an old lady on roller skates. Then, my OCD played its card, asking me, *What if you were the one who hanged him?*

By the time we reached the Columbia River Gorge, I had added so many details—the jump rope was blue, the kid was blonde, he was wearing a Scooby-Doo t-shirt—that I began to believe it had really happened and that I had been the one who'd done it.

By the time we reached my Aunt's house in Keizer, I was sure of it. I was so convinced of it that I hugged my cousin Travis and wondered if he would ever visit me in prison.

For over a month I fretted about this, each time my brain adding more and more details. Sometimes, I was able to see that it clearly wasn't real, other times I was not so sure. Finally, I was so tired of worrying that I had Andrew call the Boise Police Department and ask.

They, naturally, thought *he* was the one who was crazy.

Had I stopped ruminating over and over again about this imaginary occurrence, I could have avoided all the anxiety. But, by allowing myself to add more details, I gave it validity until there was no turning back.

So, consider this a postcard from Boise, Idaho: *Wish you were here. Stop analyzing your obsessive thoughts. The potatoes are big this time of year.*

From the start I should have added absurdities to the thoughts that continued popping into my head. I should have turned the jump rope into a giant snake and turned the little blonde boy into a tiny old man with a tattoo of Herve Villechaize on his forearm. Then, I should have just stopped analyzing it altogether.

- **Bore yourself:** If making your thoughts over the top doesn't work for you, try going for the opposite: bore yourself.

  I used to drive around our neighborhood each night, carefully searching all the houses in a mile radius for anything that was wrong: kids dying in the driveway, raging fires in bushes, people locked out of their houses in sub-zero weather.

  As I did this, I began exposing myself to the thoughts of these things happening. For a while, the more I exposed myself, the more anxious I got. But, then one day, it happened: my OCD became about as intriguing as the person at a cocktail party who talks for hours about the Dewey Decimal System.

  Exposing myself to these images gave me immunity to OCD's persuasion, leaving it boring, and powerless.

  This is the last thing OCD ever wants to be. The instant it starts to bore you, it can no longer scare you. Thus, it has no choice but to let out a frustrated huff, give you a dirty look, and, most importantly, leave you be.

- **Let go of responsibility:** One of the burdens that many of us OCDers have is an overwhelming sense of responsibility. Even as I write this sentence, I can picture my family reading it with their mouths hanging open in disbelief.

  They all think I am irresponsible. They think this because I leave my car messy and let my driver's license expire. I don't return library books on time and am always late for family dinners. But, the truth is, my mind is so filled with life and death responsibilities that I don't have room for benign, insignificant things.

Instead of caring whether my dogs are properly groomed or whether my oil is changed, I find myself absorbed in issues that, to me, matter so much more.

I find myself carefully watching the neighborhood toddlers, making sure they aren't going to wander away from home. I find myself following children in the mall, scared they might be attacked by a psychopath. I find myself lurking around ponds or creeks, ready to jump in the instant someone needs assistance.

You may have been here too. You've been so afraid that your failure to act somehow, somewhere, could cause the demise of a human being. Returning a library book has nothing on this type of responsibility.

Eventually, I had to learn that I am not responsible for everyone; it's not up to me to make sure everything's okay.

I'm not saying there aren't times when I should react. I will definitely call for help if I witness someone in need of aid. I will definitely grab the kid about to walk blindly into traffic. I will definitely ask the crying three-year-old inside the toy store if she is lost. But, I won't make it my job to intervene in all of life's potential tragedies. If I do, I will be absorbed by it.

Sometimes, everyone has to be a little selfish. Sometimes, individuals have to stop saving the world in order to simply save themselves.

- **Know your OCD might be different:** I sometimes wonder if mental illnesses are like snowflakes with no two being alike. It's important to keep that in mind and remember your OCD might be different from mine.

I have heard, for instance, that many people who have harming obsessions fear harming those closest to them:

their children or maybe the students they teach. I had these kinds of harming obsessions for a while, but they did not affect me long. The fear of harming strangers is the one that stuck around.

I am not sure why. I surely care more for the ones I love than I do strangers. But, I believe it is because my overblown concept of responsibility to protect those near and dear to me became the obsession on which I focused. I am often too busy worrying about other factors hurting those I love that I don't worry about myself being the harmer.

When I was working at the daycare, for instance, I wasn't afraid I was going to drown a kid in the pool or strangle one in the yard outside. I wasn't afraid of breaking a kid's neck or throwing one down the stairs. Instead, I was so obsessed with protecting them that I had no more room for other obsessions.

You may find this to be similar or the total opposite of your own experiences, but, no matter what, the end result is still the same: no matter who you are afraid of harming, your victims are imaginary.

- **Concentrate on the war, not the battle:** Each day that I live with OCD is a day made up of battles. Some of these battles might be minor, so restrained I hardly notice them. Other times, these battles seem intense and fiery, a surprise attack on my psyche.

  Some of these battles I win easily. I keep myself from checking. I quiet my thoughts and silence my imagination. But, other times, I will find myself believing obsessions over reality and I'll be dramatically defeated, playing General Custer to OCD's Sitting Bull.

  Yet, I remember, a bad day, a bad week, or even a bad year doesn't mean I should give up. I can lose a million battles, and still win the war.

- **Don't aim for 100 Percent:** Throughout this book, I wrote of an inability to be "100 percent sure." I couldn't be 100 percent sure I didn't start a fire or push a kid down into the lion exhibit at the local zoo.

  One of the trademarks of OCD is needing to be 100 percent sure. This makes OCD hard to defeat.

  Often, people with OCD are 99 percent sure that nothing bad has happened but have one percent full of doubt. OCD grabs that one percent and compounds it until reason disappears.

  Instead of aiming to be 100 percent sure, try being satisfied with only 99 percent—99 percent is still an A plus.

- **Know you are not alone:** I find myself, on occasion, wondering why I am stuck with this disease. But, the truth is, no life is free of pain. No matter who you are or what you have, no one is immune to suffering.

  Still, mental illness can seem like a different ballgame. There is something very isolating about it. At times I feel ashamed or embarrassed or simply think that no one in the world could possibly understand. At times I think I am the only person with these thoughts and worries. You may feel this way too.

  But, I remind myself, everyone has a little insanity. Everyone has *something*.

  My friend Steph can't sleep on a plane because she's sure that she is the only one who can keep it from crashing. My friend John can't eat vegetables or anything they touch. In college, it took my friend Keith two hours of careful study and indecision to buy a pair of pajama bottoms. My husband sometimes thinks he was abducted by aliens because he lost three hours one night when he was fourteen (I told him he probably just fell asleep).

In high school, my sister once slept downstairs because she had a "feeling" Iran was going to bomb Colorado that very night. My friend Beth used to have, what I would consider, a serious addiction to cereal. My friend Jake can't sleep unless his bedroom door is open just the right amount.

My friend Liz has a panic attack every time she passes a particular arcade on Broadway. My mom constantly follows her dog Dudley, vacuuming up the carpet paw prints he's left behind. My friend Jenny believed in the Easter Bunny until her parents staged an intervention to convince her he wasn't real. She was seventeen at the time.

See. It isn't just you or just me. It's all of us. In the end, in some way, we're all crazy.

Some people just don't know it yet.

Your friend,

J. J. Keeler